Pithy Quotes

Designed to Improve Your Bottom Line or, At the Least, Your Disposition

Pithy Quotes

Designed to Improve Your Bottom Line or, At the Least, Your Disposition

Chairman Carter's Collection
Volume X

***BOOK*LOGIX®**

BOOKLOGIX®
Alpharetta, Georgia

All rights reserved. No part of this book may be reproduced or transmitted in any form or by any means, electronic or mechanical, including photocopying, recording, or any information storage and retrieval system, without permission in writing from the publisher.

Pithy Quotes
Chairman Carter's Collection
10th Edition, Volume XI
www.Businessquotes.com

Copyright © 2013 by Bud Carter
Paperback edition December 2013

ISBN: 978-1-61005-450-8   20131127

Cover Design by Christopher North, Spring Publishing, Reporter Newspapers (reporternewspapers.net)
Printed in the United States of America

∞ This paper meets the requirements of ANSI/NISO Z39.48-1992 (Permanence of Paper)

For corrections of attribution please go to businessquotes.com

Table of Contents

Pit Bull Management…	1
You Just Don't Understand…	25
The Unfair Advantage…	55
In Search of the Magic Bullet…	73
How to Make Penguins Fly…	99
Sliding Down the Razor Blade of Life…	121
Slaying Life's Goliaths…	145
Let's Get Serious About Humo	161
Index…	181

Preface

More than 26 years now, I've had the pleasure of hearing some very bright people discuss one of my favorite subjects: the business of business. And because that's the way I'm wired, early on I found myself jotting down their salient snippets, a well turned phrase that, in a very few words, gave an idea, a concept, broad meaning and impact.

Maurice Mascarenhas was one of the first. Speaking of the responsibility of CEOs, he said, "You never pick up the paper and read 'passengers crash airplane." In less than a dozen words, he helped my CEO members understand the scope of their responsibility, the impact, the person in the corner office should have.

Over the years, my members and I have heard hundreds of speakers on topics ranging from Finance, Sales, and Presentation Skills to HR, Marketing, and Stress Management, hopefully gaining wisdom from each. The first edition of this book was printed back when Vistage was TEC and I was responsible for helping grow the Southeast. This is now Volume X. In the late 90s the brass in San Diego made that edition their holiday gift and more than 9,000 were sent out not only here in this country, but to members in Australia, Canada and the United Kingdom as well.

My members have grown used to seeing the month's applicable pithy quotes on the walls at their meetings and in their meeting folders; and I'm still flattered seeing them posted in their break rooms, hallways and offices.

I've been asked as to my favorites and will suggest several because I believe they are great examples of how so much can be communicated in so few words. Vistage legend Jim Cecil's cleared any confusion away about Sales and Marketing when he explained, "Sales picks the low hanging fruit; Marketing waters the tree." Peter Schutz is remembered for cautioning that "If you'll listen closely, your customers will explain your business to you." More recently, Michael Canic cut to the core, noting, "If you can't change the people, change the people."

So here it is… with thanks not only to the speakers and business publications who provided the content, but to first member ever Russ Walden (a #150 member since 1987) for his critical review, and, with a deep waist bow and unlimited appreciation, to best friend and wife Kay for the countless hours she spent creating order out of my chaos, proof reading and making sure the quotes said to be on a specific page were really there.

Thanks to the crew at BookLogix who reformatted this book and helped create and publish an outstanding book.

I hope you enjoy the book and will forward your favorite Pithy Quote, your best Salient Snippet, just in case there is a Volume XI.

Bud Carter

Budcarter@aol.com

Pit Bull Management

I

Terse commentary providing laser focus insight how no nonsense, bottom line driven management behaves – or should.

Don't cheat your people out of the opportunity to win because of your discomfort holding people accountable.
—*Michael Canic* Vistage Speaker

Revenue is vanity, margin is sanity, and cash is king.
—*Unknown*

The factory of the future will have but two employees...a man and a dog. The man will be there to feed the dog. The dog will be there to keep the man from touching the equipment.
—*Warren Bennis* Educator

As it turns out, plants and dollars can be managed, but people expect leadership.
—*D. Wayne Calloway* PepsiCo

No manager ever gives a bad territory to a top performer.
—*Gil Cargill* Vistage Speaker

In looking for people to hire, you look for three qualities: integrity, intelligence and energy. And if they don't have the first, the other two will kill you.
—*Warren Buffet* Industrialist

Looking for a place where price is not a factor is going to be a long, lonely search in dark jungles.
—*Sam Bowers* Vistage Speaker

Recessions create a huge opportunity for the healthy.
—*Austen Jackson* Rising Tide

If you don't value what you do for your customer, they won't either.
—*Jaynie Smith* Vistage Speaker

Fair is a feeling, not a fact.
—*Kraig Kramers* Vistage Speaker

Conflict in most organizations is phony and designed to relieve people of having to take a risk and do anything significant.
—**Dr. Jerry Harvey** *Vistage Speaker*

Power is having options and a willingness to take risks.
—**Jack Kaine** *Vistage Speaker*

We've got so many problems we can't help but solve some.
—**David Hanson** *SyncroFlo*

Pain drives change.
—**Robert Rodriquez** *Innovation Network*

Goals produce results, not activities.
—**John McNeil** *Vistage Speaker*

The sting of change is nothing compared to the pain of obsolescence.
—**Unknown**

Poor execution will eat good strategy for breakfast every day.
—**Dan Barnett** *Vistage Speaker*

If you haven't restructured your company in the past three years you're in trouble. A company is not a Catholic marriage - forever. It's California style - one year at a time.
—**Ichak Adizes** *Consultant*

If you're not growing your company at 18%, go play golf
—**Richard Rodnick** *Geneva Group*

Enterprises are paid to create wealth, not control costs.
—**Peter Drucker** *Educator*

Don't bring me an order, bring me a customer.
—**Eli Goldratt** *Consultant*

The most expensive time in a manager's life is the time between when you truly lose faith in someone and when you do something about it.
—*Jack Daly*   Vistage Speaker

Leaders don't matter that much. They are like light bulbs: you've just got to find one that works.
—*Robert Sutton*   Educator

The primary reason the turnaround industry exists today is the failure of top level management to make tough decisions in a timely manner.
—*Jeff Vogelsang*   Vistage Speaker

If something cannot go on forever, it will stop.
—*Herbert Stein*   Economist

Intolerable performance exists when intolerable performance is tolerated.
—*Dennis Snow*   Vistage Speaker

Good enough is never good enough.
—*Jack Welch*   General Electric

A brilliant executive is the one who can spot a pattern with the fewest possible facts.
—*Fred Adler*   Author

When setting goals, it is important to remember that the individual controls only his own effort, not the product, the economy or the competition.
—*Renn Zaphiropoulos*   Vistage Speaker

If you find yourself replacing one underperformer…with another underperformer…with another underperformer, and wondering why you can't find any good employees anymore, take a look in the mirror and ask, 'What's the only variable here that hasn't changed?'
—*Vicki Schneider*   Vistage Chairman

I am not interested in excuses for delay. I am only interested in things done.
—**Nehru** *Government Leader*

The plan is nothing; planning is everything.
—**Gen. Dwight D. Eisenhower** *President*

The only thing worse than training your employees and losing them is not training your employees and keeping them.
—**Zig Ziglar** *Trainer*

Don't tell me about the storms you encountered - did you bring in the ship?
—**Unknown**

The worst thing we can do is do the wrong thing well.
—**Irwin Miller** *Cummins Engine*

The riches are in the niches.
— **Roger Blackwell** *Vistage Speaker*

No person can get very far in this life on a 40 hour week.
—**J.W. Marriott** *Marriott Hotels*

Unhappy people attract other unhappy people and in a small company that can kill you.
—**Charlie King** *King Industrial Realty*

If you have a morale problem, it relates to some inconsistency in your organization.
—**Hunter Lott** *Vistage Speaker*

Opportunity and need equal greed.
—**Unknown**

Failing organizations are usually over managed and under led.
—**Warren Bennis,** *Educator*

Everyone has a plan - until he gets hit.
—**Mike Tyson** *Boxer*

You don't want to be in a commodity business unless you're the biggest, meanest kid on the block and you have the lowest price.
—*Jerry Goldress* *Vistage Speaker*

You can't build a reputation on what you're going to do.
—**Henry Ford** *Industrialist*

Leaders are not paid to make the inevitable happen.
—**Vince Langley** *Vistage Speaker*

Execute or be executed.
—**Randy Fretz** *Wells Real Estate Funds*

No one buying your company wants to be married to you.
—*James Erben* *Vistage Speaker*

In this flatter world where most managers have a broader span of control, there aren't enough hours in the day to double-check everything employees do.
—*Scott Flanders* *Columbia House*

When placed in competition for contracts, he who knows the least, bids the least.
—**Bob Ellery** *Sierra Pacific Industries*

In a small business, the most important decisions you make are the things you decide not to do.
—**Unknown**

Flex hours are wonderful for people in an orchestra.
— **Renn Zaphiropoulos** *Vistage Speaker*

If you can't change the people, change the people.
— **Michael Canic** *Vistage Speaker*

Excuses and results are mutually exclusive.
—*Jim Bleech*   Vistage Speaker

We reward with our attention those people who are doing what we do not want them to do.
—**Lee Ozley**   Vistage Speaker

Rework is evil.
—**Bob Patterson**   Boeing

The leader must know, must know that he knows, and must be able to make it abundantly clear to those about him that he knows.
—**Clarence B. Randall**   Industrialist

Teamwork is not a goal of your business it is a means to accomplish goals.
—**Will Phillips**   Vistage Speaker

If you don't make dust, you eat it.
—**Bernard Marcus**   Home Depot

Good management consists of showing average people how to do the work of superior people.
—**John D. Rockefeller Sr**   Standard Oil

The conditions necessary to cause your largest client to disappear are in place and have been activated.
—**Sam Bowers**   Vistage Speaker

Start-ups: Take small bite. Chew well. Swallow. Repeat.
—**Om Malik**   Author

Before you commit to going to Hell and back, make sure you emphasize the getting back part.
—**Bud Mingledorff**   Mingledorff's

Venture capitalists buy into pipe dreams all the time - they call them business plans.
—**Russ Walden**   Ridgewood Properties

If you wait until you need cash to get cash, it's too late.
—**Don Hankey** *Hankey Group*

Moaning is not a management task.
—**Rupert Stadler** *Audi*

If you want to be the first into a new territory, you cannot wait for a large amount of evidence.
—***Joel A. Barker*** *Consultant*

When you meet miserable, unhappy whiney, employees, blame their boss.
—**Hunter Lott** *Vistage Speaker*

Insanity is doing the same thing over and over again and expecting different results.
—***Albert Einstein*** *Physicist*

If you can't solve a problem, make it bigger.
—**Donald Rumsfeld** *Secretary of Defense*

If you think all your customers are created equally, you're headed for bankruptcy.
— **Jim Cecil** *Vistage Speaker*

Only the paranoid survive.
—**Andy Grove** *Intel*

The telling difference between companies in an industry is what they do when things go wrong.
—**Bud Mingledorff** *Mingledorff's*

Success seems to be largely a matter of hanging on after others have let go.
—**Leonard Feather** *Journalist*

If you have too many problems, maybe you should go out of business. There is no law that says a company must last forever.
—**Peter Drucker** *Educator*

Problems are created when reality is avoided. Great leaders talk about the tough topics.
—**Pat Murray** *Vistage Speaker*

Recognize efforts; reward results.
—**Catherine Meek** *Vistage Speaker*

Require commitment not compliance.
—**Richard Teerlink** *Harley-Davidson*

Culture eats strategy for breakfast.
—**Mark Fields** *Ford Motor Company*

Long range planning does not deal with future decisions, but the future of present decisions.
—**Peter Drucker** *Educator*

The reason Marketing exists is to make it easier for Sales to sell.
—**Jeff Fisher** *I.B.I.S.*

You're not a real manager unless you've been sacked.
—**Malcolm Allison** *Author*

The one rule of business today is that there are no rules.
—**Ira Blumenthal** *Vistage Speaker*

Integrity matters.
—**Andy Vabulas** *I.B.I.S.*

A friendship founded on business is a good deal better than a business founded on friendship.
—**John D. Rockefeller Sr** *Standard Oil*

In your business decisions, risk only money…never people or relationships.
—**Jack DeBoer** *ValuePlace*

Too many companies let bad leaders hide behind good numbers.
—**Richard Hadden** *Vistage Speaker*

It's not the employer who pays the wages. Employers only handle the money. It's the customer who pays the wages.
—**Henry Ford** *Industrialist*

Today's great companies are professionally managed and entrepreneurially driven.
—***Jerry Goldress*** *Vistage Speaker*

Boldness in business is the first, second and third thing.
—***Thomas Fuller*** *Religious Leader*

To live through an impossible situation you don't need the reflexes of a Grand Prix driver, the muscles of Hercules, nor the mind of Einstein. You simply need to know what to do.
—**Anthony Greenbank** *Author*

Without knowing where you are at all times financially, you are destined to fail.
—***Dean Austin*** *Wyngate Int.*

At the end of the day you bet on people, not strategies.
—***Lawrence Bossidy*** *Allied Signal*

The smarter we think we are, the more likely we are to discount information that doesn't fit with what we know.
—***Deanna Berg*** *Vistage Speaker*

You should invest in a business that even a fool can run, because some day a fool will.
—***Warren Buffet*** *Industrialist*

The best way to cope with change is to help create it.
—***Robert Dole*** *Senator*

A wrong decision can always be corrected. Lost time you can never get back.
—***Jan Carlzon*** *Scandinavian Airlines*

Courage is being scared to death and saddling up anyway.
—*John Wayne* *Actor*

The best way to keep a good employee is to fire a bad one.
—**Bob Thomson** *Vistage Speaker*

Simply refusing to spend, in the hope that this is the safe thing to do, is hardly inspired.
—**Kerry Sulkowicz,** *Industrial Psychologist*

What kills a company is that stuff that is so quiet, so low profile, so off the screen, that you never see it.
—**Donald Phinn** *Vistage Speaker*

One should forgive one's enemies, but not before they are hanged.
—**Henrich Heine** *Poet*

Important and relevant are not the same thing
—**Brad Remillard,** *Vistage Speaker*

The stupid and the greedy will always meet.
—**Dave Ramsey** *Talk Show Host*

Your choice as a CEO is to work hard or hire smart.
—**Bob Prosen** *Vistage Speaker*

The first clean kill awakes the herd.
—**Dr. Mark Rumans** *Clinician*

You never pay anybody too much, but you might pay them too long.
—**Jack Hardin** *Attorney*

Yours will become a learning organization - one way or the other.
—**Howard Hyden** *Vistage Speaker*

A decision is a judgment. It is a choice between alternatives. It is at best a choice between "almost right" and "probably wrong."
—*Peter Drucker* *Educator*

Your business is a project; simply something to get done with.
—*Michael Gerber* *Author*

Don't leave before you leave.
—*Sheryl Sandberg* *Facebook*

The basic responsibility of the CEO is to design the game and arrange the talent.
—*Renn Zaphiropoulos* *Vistage Speaker*

Management's biggest problem is all the unemployed people on the payroll.
—*Unknown*

Money loves speed.
—*Joe Vitale* *Executive Mentoring*

Adequate performance gets a generous severance package.
—*Reed Hastings* *Netflix*

The failure of most people in a work-out is not working on the top line.
—*Lee Katz* *Grisanti, Galef & Goldress*

I'll take 50% efficiency to get 100% loyalty.
—*Samuel Goldwyn* *Businessman*

Do not ask the question till you know what you are going to do with the answer.
—*John Kay* *Economist*

Leadership is one of the things you cannot delegate. You either exercise it or you abdicate it.
—*Robert Goizueta* *Coca-Cola*

No agenda, no meeting.
— *Bruce Breier*   *Vistage Speaker*

Always forgive your enemies, but never forget their names.
—*Robert F. Kennedy*   *Attorney General*

Silence isn't always golden you know. Sometimes it's plain yellow.
—*Jan Kemp*   *Author*

Good credit is for sissies.
—*Vincent Forsee*   *Link-Systems Intl.*

The second you get an inkling somebody is not working out, you're already late.
—*Jerry Goldress*   *Vistage Speaker*

Occasionally people succeed because they are brilliant and visionary; mostly it's because they work harder than anyone else.
—*Michael Eisner*   *Disney Company*

The surest way to achieve strategic surprise is to do something absolutely stupid.
—*Gen. Dwight D. Eisenhower*   *President*

Most businesses grow themselves into trouble.
—*Gerry Faust*   *Vistage Speaker*

The concept of "value added" will drive more companies bankrupt than any other.
—*Sam Bowers*   *Vistage Speaker*

Don't spend your time on anything your customers don't perceive to be of value.
—*Michael Basch*   *Vistage Speaker*

There is nothing more dangerous than a small man working for a big company.
—*Sean Casten*   *Turbostream Corp.*

When you're going through Hell, keep going.
—**Winston Churchill**   Government Leader

The most expensive thing you have in your business is capacity excess.
—**Sam Bowers**   Vistage Speaker

Management's challenge is to sell more with fewer people to customers who demand more service and attention for less money.
—**Jim Cecil**   Vistage Speaker

Never let a crisis go to waste.
—**Fareed Zakaria,**   Journalist

Whenever you say, 'I could have', 'I should have', or 'I would have', it means you didn't.
—**Michael Canic**   Vistage Speaker

The bottom line is the bottom line.
—**Bud Carter**   Vistage Chairman

If we want to maintain the quality, the integrity and the whole culture of our company, we've got to own it.
—**Truett Cathy**   Chick-Fil-A

There is no data on the future.
—**Laurel Cutler**   Advertising Executive

Never attempt to murder a man who is committing suicide.
—**Woodrow Wilson**   US President

If you're going to be stupid you've got to be tough.
—**Unknown**

Although your customers won't love you if you give bad service, your competitors will.
—**Kate Zabriskie**   Business Training Works

A leader is a dealer in hope.
—**Napoleon Bonaparte**   Government Leader

Everything you say as CEO is like whispering through a megaphone.
—**Steve Yastrow** *Vistage Speaker*

When we should, we do.
—**David Calhoun** *Larson-Juhl*

If everyone agrees with you they probably don't mean it.
—**Unknown**

Most companies grow themselves out of business. They either can't finance it or they can't manage it.
—**Richard Palmer** *Vistage Speaker*

A team effort is a lot of people doing what I say.
—**Michael Winner** *Film Director*

If your company was a ship, a good CFO would be in the bow charting the course, not on the stern recording the wake.
—**Unknown**

The first word in merger is 'me.'
—**Bud Mingledorff** *Mingledorff's*

The first method for estimating the intelligence of a ruler is to look at the men he has around him.
—**Machiavelli** *Philosopher*

Don't ever forget what you knew when you were one of the boys.
—**Renn Zaphiropoulos** *Vistage Speaker*

When there's no penalty for failure, failure proliferates.
—**George Will** *Journalist*

A problem that can be solved with money is just an expense.
—**Trip Van Roden** *Wellspring*

Pit Bull Management

Use your spies for every kind of business.
 —**Sun Tzu** *Philosopher*

The purpose of your organization is to meet customer needs. That's the game. Profits are the score.
 —**Clark Wigley** *Vistage Speaker*

Budgets are not a mandatory license to spend.
 —**John Shiely** *Briggs & Stratton*

If you have negative, destructive people in your organization —there is but one question, why?
 — **Jay Refinbary** *Vistage speaker*

Profit is the current value of past performance.
 —**Clark Wigley** *Vistage Speaker*

There is a point at which your will defines your capability.
 —**David Taylor-Klaus** *Digital Positions*

If you pick the right people and give them the opportunity to spread their wings, and put compensation as a carrier behind it, you almost don't have to manage them.
 —**Jack Welch** *General Electric*

Trust your gut, don't cover your butt; they pay you to do what is right.
 —**Paul Richards** *Baseball Executive*

The two deadliest enemies of any business are arrogance and ignorance.
 —**Jack Stack** *SRC Holdings*

Never interrupt the enemy when he is doing something wrong.
 —**Erwin Rommel** *Military Leader*

Ethics are non-negotiable.
 —**Russ Walden** *Ridgewood Properties*

The buck stops with the guy who writes the checks.
—**Rupert Murdoch** *Industrialist*

Survival has a strange way of consuming one's attention and energy.
—**Kirby Martzall** *Vistage Chairman*

Leaders get paid to make choices.
—**Pat Murray** *Vistage Speaker*

Having lots of money doesn't change anything. It just amplifies it. Jerks become bigger jerks and nice guys become nicer.
—**Ben Narasin** *Businessman*

The work to get to 'easy' isn't.
—**Danica Patrick** *Race Car Driver*

We don't have time, as leaders, to babysit adults.
—**Jay Refinbary** *Vistage Speaker*

Eat more nails for breakfast.
—**Randy Morgan** *Westone Labs*

Pay for results. Pay for performance, but don't pay for effort.
—**Ralph Parilla** *Vistage Speaker*

The things that got you to where you are today are not the things that will get you to the future.
—**Peter Drucker** *Educator*

Length of service should not guarantee continued employment.
—**Emory Mulling** *Vistage Speaker*

We can't operate ourselves to a profit anymore; we have to grow the top line.
—**Tom Feltenstein** *Vistage Speaker*

Selling is simple - it's not easy, but it is simple.
—**Fred Herman** *Consultant*

It's best to be Atilla the Hun every day rather than every other day.
—**Richard Palmer** *Vistage Speaker*

If you do not know the answer to a question, give yourself time to think about it by asking that the question be repeated.
—**Barney Goldberg** *Gateway Sporting Goods Co.*

One major obligation is not to mistake slogans for solutions.
—**Edward R. Murrow** *Journalist*

Anyone can lead when a mandate appears. The real leader emerges in a situation of ambiguity.
—**James Newton** *Vistage Speaker*

You are not your target market.
—**Jim Cecil** *Vistage Speaker*

The toleration of mediocrity by the CEO does more to hold back a company than any other factor.
—**Larry King** *Vistage Speaker*

A turkey on your plate is a lot easier to digest than one on your payroll.
—**Jack Daly** *Vistage Speaker*

The leader's job is not to cover all the bases - it is to see that all the bases are covered.
—**James Crupi** *Strategic Leadership Solutions*

The purpose of business is to create and keep a customer.
—**Peter Drucker** *Educator*

A budget is not a bank account.
—**Scott Smith** *La Plata Investments*

Generals don't belong in the trenches.
—**David Hauseman** *The Hauseman Group*

There is the risk you cannot afford to take, and there is the risk you cannot afford not to take.
—**Peter Drucker** *Educator*

It's entirely possible that ignorance is our only renewable resource.
—**Bill Cobb** *Vistage Speaker*

Bigger isn't better if it isn't making money.
—**Pat Flinn** *ValueJet*

It is only when we develop others that we permanently succeed.
—**Harvey Firestone** *Industrialist*

Managing is like holding a dove in your hand. Squeeze too hard and you kill it; not hard enough and it flies away.
—**Tommy Lasorda** *Baseball Manager*

Stay away from the courthouse; you'll never make any money there.
—**J.E. Davis** *Winn-Dixie*

Nothing is more wasteful than doing with the greatest of efficiency that which should not be done in the first place.
—**Ted Levitt** *Hayward Daily Review*

It is not necessary to change. Survival is not mandatory.
—**W. Edwards Deming** *Educator*

Every normal man must be tempted at times to spit upon his hands, hoist the black flag, and begin slitting throats.
—**Henry Louis Mencken** *Humorist*

Credit is the lubricant of commerce. It's not an Accounting function; it's a Sales function.
—**Abe Sanchez** *Vistage Speaker*

Leadership is not paid to make the inevitable happen.
—**Lauch McKinnon** *RockBridge Commercial Bank*

The essentials to successful management are good people, goals, roles and rules.
—**Will Phillips** *Vistage Speaker*

At the point you're sick and tired of saying it, it'll be at the point where they're just about to get it.
—**Greg Bustin,** *Vistage Speaker*

As managers we have to get out of the behavior modification business.
—**Ed Ryan** *Vistage Speaker*

The janitor gets to explain why something went wrong. Senior management does not.
—**Steve Jobs** *Apple*

There is no trying; there is doing or not doing.
—**Jorge Posada** *Baseball Player*

There are only three truths in business: cash flow, the P&L, and the balance sheet.
—**John Rice** *HR Access*

A goal is a dream with a deadline.
—**Harvey Mackay** *Author*

Accountability requires consequences. You can't have one without the other.
—**Don Schmincke** *Vistage Speaker*

Your business can't afford the word can't.
—**Del Poling** *Vistage Speaker*

"Why" is not a word used by effective management?
—**Charles Lipman** *DiversiTech*

Don't wait until you're drowning to put up your hand.
—**Val Dempsey** *CEI*

The whole business of business today is to reduce inventory and increase inventory turns.
—**Dave Duryee** *Vistage Speaker*

Never "for the sake of peace and quiet" deny your own experience or convictions.
—**Dag Hammarskjold** *United Nations*

Thrift is the new extravagance.
—**David Houle** *Vistage Speaker*

There is no such thing as a fixed cost.
—**Jerry Goldress** *Vistage Speaker*

There's nothing that cleanses your soul like getting the hell kicked out of you.
—**Woody Hayes** *Football Coach*

The goal is The Goal; everything else is a variable.
—**Howard Hyden** *Vistage Speaker*

Production minus Sales equals scrap.
—**Jay Levinson** *Author*

Hire character. Train skill.
—**Peter Schutz** *Porsche*

While you're saving face you're losing your ass.
—**Lyndon B. Johnson** *President*

When you play defense, you have to win 100% of the time - and you can't.
—**Herb Meyer** *Vistage Speaker*

Pit Bull Management

Safe trumps cheap.
— **Gerry Layo,** *Vistage Speaker*

Rules without relationships lead to rebellion.
—**Jerry Manuel** *Baseball Manager*

Crises create opportunity.
—**Jeff McCart** *The McCart Group*

If you're the 800 pound gorilla in your market and you're not stepping on the competition, you're missing the point.
—**Gideon Malherbe** *Vistage Speaker*

Consumers are statistics. Customers are people.
—**Stanley Marcus** *Neiman Marcus*

Policies are many; principles are few; policies will change, principles never do.
—**John Maxwell, Author**

If there is no change there is no need to manage.
—**Peter Schutz** *Vistage Speaker*

The pain of uncertainty is much worse than the certainty of pain.
—**Frank Maguire** *Vistage Speaker*

Get out of the near successes; those products and services drain a business.
—**Peter Drucker** *Educator*

Nothing focuses the mind like a hanging in the morning.
—**Wyatt Earp** *Lawman*

You Just Don't Understand

II

Some things are obvious,
but only from the other side of the desk.

You Just Don't Understand...

A career is a wonderful thing but you can't snuggle up to it on a cold night.
—**Marilyn Monroe**   *Entertainer*

Life is what happens to you when you are making other plans.
—**Betty Talmadge**   **Political Leader**

No one has a picture of their boss hanging on their wall at home.
—**Lynn Rose**   **The Seydel Company**

After all is said and done, more is said than done.
—**Amy K Hutchens**   *Vistage Speaker*

If no one took risks, Michelangelo would have painted the Sistine floor.
—**Neil Simon**   *Playwright*

All selling is about trust.
—**Duane Lakin**   *Vistage Speaker*

Although reasonable people do disagree, if we do, that will not be my first thought.
—**Charles Lipman**   *DiversiTech*

If it's common, it's not wisdom — and if it's wisdom, it's not common.
—**Herb Kelleher**   *Southwest Airlines*

Crash programs fail because they are based on the theory that with nine women pregnant you can get a baby a month.
—**Wernher Von Braun**   *Scientist*

An agreement is nothing but a license to negotiate.
—**Tom Wood**   *Vistage Speaker*

Bad administration can destroy good policy; but good administration can never save bad policy.
—**Adlai Stevenson** *Governor*

There isn't any customer satisfaction without employee satisfaction.
—**Gordon Bethune** *Continental Airlines*

Any mistake you survive is a learning experience.
—**Bud Mingledorff** *Mingledorff's*

Bureaucracy defends the status quo long past the time the quo has lost its status.
—**Laurence J. Peter** *Educator*

A CEO may be a fool and fail to know it, but not if the shares of his company are publicly traded.
—**Katherine Westcott**

By working faithfully eight hours a day you may eventually get to be a boss and work 12 hours a day.
—**Robert Frost** *Poet*

The longer a customer has a problem, the bigger it gets.
—**C. Leslie Charles** *Consultant*

Entrepreneurship is the pursuit of opportunity without regard to resources currently controlled.
—**Howard Stevenson** *HBS*

Cash ain't cash unless it's cash.
—**Red Scott** *Vistage Speaker*

You can't frighten people into feeling safe.
—**Joe Cotrozolla** *Vistage Chairman*

Children don't take after strangers.
—**John Lee** *Vistage Speaker*

You Just Don't Understand…

All organizations are in transition whether they know it or not.
—**Eric Flamholtz** *Educator*

Coincidence is God's way of staying anonymous.
—**Steven Snyder** *Vistage Speaker*

Customers don't want choices; they want exactly what they want.
—**Joseph Pine** *Aurora*

Don't encourage humility in your people. Humility is a very neurotic emotion.
—**Morrie Shechtman** *Vistage Speaker*

Eagles may soar, but weasels don't get sucked into jet engines.
—**John Benfield** *Businessman*

Any excuse will serve a tyrant.
—**Aesop** *Philosopher*

No business, no problems. No problems, no business, Problems are opportunities for solutions.
—**George Naddaff** *Boston Chicken*

A customer's desire to be treated with respect and have their business appreciated is the only "fixed" in the variable world of business.
—**Clark Johnson** *Vistage Speaker*

Efforts and courage are not enough without purpose.
—**John F. Kennedy** *President*

Failure is only the opportunity to begin again more intelligently.
—**Henry Ford** *Industrialist*

Judgment wanes as the check book grows.
—**David Calhoun** *Larson-Juhl*

Fatigue makes cowards of us all.
—**Vince Lombardi** *Football Coach*

I'd rather get shot in the face attacking a problem than shot in the back running away from one.
—**Scott Sorrell** *Vistage Speaker*

First things first; second things never.
—**Eliza Patton Ross**

The difference between a job and a career is the difference between 40 and 60 hours a week.
—**Robert Frost** *Poet*

Freedom is greatest when the rules for behavior are clear and enforced.
—**Plato** *Philosopher*

Gun fighters are not paid by the bullet.
—**Joe Geary** *Dallas Attorney*

Criticism is the disapproval of people, not for having faults, but for having faults different from their own.
—**Unknown**

Great minds discuss ideas; average minds discuss events; small minds discuss people.
—**Eleanor Roosevelt** *U.N. Delegate*

A relationship is not something that you pursue; it's what happens to you when you are immersed in serving the dreams of your customer.
—**Tom Peters** *Author*

Great wealth is created during periods of great crises.
—**Robert Balentine** *Balentine*

What lies hidden in the chiefs breeds' monsters in the tribe.
—**Andy Fleming** *Vistage Speaker*

You Just Don't Understand…

Hierarchy is an organization with its face toward the CEO and its ass toward the customer.
—**Jack Welch**   *General Electric*

A reputation is easier kept than recovered.
—**Randy Fretz**   *Wells Real Estate Funds*

I am a leader, therefore I must follow.
—**Voltaire**   *Philosopher*

Discretionary bonuses are the tool of management too lazy to identify the factors driving significant business success.
—**Andy Vabulas**   *IBIS*

I am extraordinarily patient provided I get my own way in the end.
—**Margaret Thatcher**   *Prime Minister*

It is easier to resist at the beginning than at the end.
—**Leonardo Da Vinci**   *Artist*

You can't order change.
—**Jim McNemey**   *Boeing*

I have never heard of a dying man asking for another day to go to the office.
—**Maurice Mascarenhas**   *Vistage Speaker*

I wish I could stand on a busy corner, hat in hand and beg people to throw me all their wasted hours.
—**Bernard Berenson**   *Critic*

If you're always focusing on results you're always focused on the past - the lagging instead of leading indicators.
—**Dan Barnett**   *Vistage Speaker*

Among the chief worries of today's business executives is the large number of unemployed still on the payrolls.
—*Unknown*

If the meteorologists started forecasting the economy, and economists took a turn at predicting the weather, I doubt the accuracy of either endeavor would diminish.
—*The Vent*   Atlanta Journal Constitution

You're not truly successful as a CEO until a client calls and you have no idea what he's talking about.
—*Walt Kiser*   Law Engineering

When your ship comes in make sure you are willing to unload it.
—*Robert Anthony*   Author

I'd rather be sorry for something I did than for something I didn't do.
—*Red Scott*   Vistage Speaker

The function of leadership is to produce more leaders, not followers.
—*Ralph Nader*   Consumer Advocate

If I had known what it would cost me to have it all, I would have settled for less.
—*Lily Tomlin*   Entertainer

The purpose of getting our folks to join organizations is not to get them to know everybody; it's to get everybody to know them.
—*Charlie King*   King Industrial Realty

In a fight between you and the world, bet on the world.
—*Franz Kafka*   Author

You Just Don't Understand...

Agreement is a problem. Once we agree with others we have to share their risk.
—**Dr. Jerry Harvey** *Vistage Speaker*

If I say something which you understand fully in this regard, I probably made a mistake.
—**Allan Greenspan** *Federal Reserve*

Most people don't need a boss; they need someone to listen to them.
—**Maurice Mascarenhas** *Vistage Speaker*

If it's a really big deal, your sales people will screw it up.
—**Tom Searcy** *Vistage Speaker*

Procrastination means paying twice the price when eventually you must act.
—**T.A. McAloon**

If there's a 50/50 chance something can go wrong, then nine times out of ten it will.
—**Paul Harvey** *Commentator*

People don't know how to buy, they know how to price.
—**Gerry Layo** *Vistage Speaker*

Consensus is the absence of leadership.
—**Margaret Thatcher** *Prime Minister*

If two people always agree, one of them is not necessary.
—**Deanna Berg** *Vistage Speaker*

In order to succeed, you must know what you are doing, like what you are doing, and believe in what you are doing.
—**Will Rogers** *Humorist*

A fanatic is one who can't change his mind and won't change the subject.
   —**Winston Churchill** *Government Leader*

We can always overestimate the change that will occur in the next two years and underestimate the change that will occur in the next ten. Don't let yourself be lulled into inaction.
   —**Bill Gates** *Microsoft*

A monologue is not a decision.
   —**Clement Atlee** *Government Leader*

Lack of planning on your part does not constitute a crisis on my part.
   —**Peter Ueberroth** *NFL*

It's not work unless you'd rather be doing something else.
   —**Walt Sessoms** *Bell South*

Don't compromise yourself. You're all you've got.
   —**Janis Joplin** *Entertainer*

Speak when you are angry and you will have made the best speech you'll ever regret.
   —**Laurence J. Peter** *Educator*

In a crowded marketplace, fitting in is failing - and not standing out is to be invisible.
   —**Tom Feltenstein** *Vistage Speaker*

It's hard to make money when you're trying to make a living.
   —**Bill Blanton** *First Capital Bank*

Good is not good, when better is expected.
   —**Thomas Fuller** *Religious Leader*

You Just Don't Understand...

Information is not knowledge and knowledge is not wisdom.
—**Ken Ruscio** *Washington & Lee University*

It has been my experience that men who have no vices have very few virtues.
—**Abraham Lincoln** *President*

It's hard to boss your buddies.
—**Leo Wells** *Wells Real Estate Funds*

A conclusion is simply the place where you got tired of thinking.
—**Unknown**

If you can dream it, you can live it.
—**Walt Disney** *Industrialist*

It's hard to compete with free. Free and "good enough" beats costly and technically elegant any day.
—**Andrew Jaquith** *The Yankee Group*

Leaders get their kicks from organizing the work of others - not from doing it themselves.
—**Dick Cook** *Vistage Speaker*

If you owe the bank a little money, you have a problem; if you owe the bank a lot of money, they have a problem.
—**Russ Walden** *Ridgewood Properties*

Those not fired with enthusiasm will be fired with enthusiasm.
—**Vince Lombardi** *Football Coach*

Life is like a dogsled team. If you ain't the lead dog the scenery never changes.
—**Lewis Grizzard** *Columnist*

An interview with a prospective employee is like prom night - it just doesn't get any better.
—**Barry Shamis** *Vistage Speaker*

There is nothing more dangerous to an organization than a leader who is under employed.
—**Pat Murray** *Vistage Speaker*

Life is like a sewer. You get out of it what you put into it.
—**Tom Lehrer** *Satirist*

If men did not put their responsibilities above everything else, the bulk of lovemaking wouldn't be done at night.
—**Henry S. Haskins** *Author*

My greatest strength as a consultant is to be ignorant and ask a few questions.
—**Peter Drucker** *Educator*

Luck is the dividend of sweat. The more you sweat the luckier you get.
—**Ray Kroc** *McDonalds*

Kicking the tree does not hasten the ripening.
—**Jim Cecil** *Vistage Speaker*

All the animals except man know the principal business of life is to enjoy it.
—**Samuel Butler** *Poet*

If your people can get to work by 8 and go home by 5 and do their job without thinking, they are already obsolete.
—**Gideon Malherbe** *Vistage Speaker*

You Just Don't Understand...

When you live on cash, you understand the limits of the world around which you navigate each day. Credit leads into a desert with invisible boundaries.
—**Anton Chekhov** *Author*

You are only as competent as the weakest key executive who reports to you.
—**Maurice Mascarenhas** *Vistage Speaker*

Men are conservative when they are least vigorous or when they are most luxurious.
—**Ralph Waldo Emerson** *Author*

If you don't ask, you don't get.
—**Joe Shore** *Communications Channel*

Most organizations are perfectly designed to solve yesterday's problems not to capitalize on tomorrow's opportunities.
—**Linda Honold** *Vistage Speaker*

College prepared me for a world that doesn't exist.
—**Nashville Vistage Member**

Only mediocrities rise to the top in a system that won't tolerate wave making.
—**Laurence J. Peter** *Educator*

Lower your price enough and your better customers will leave you.
—**Chuck Reaves** *Vistage Speaker*

Managers promote stability while Leaders press for change; and only organizations that embrace both sides of that contradiction can thrive in turbulent times.
—**Verne Harnishe** *Journalist*

Your company's culture is the unspoken way stuff gets done.
—**Bob Prosen** *Vistage Speaker*

Mediocrity is so easily achieved that there is no point planning for it.
—**Lee Sechrest** *Educator*

Meetings are the Rodney Dangerfields of organizations, they get no respect.
—**Clark Wigley** *Vistage Speaker*

The difference between the way you look and how you see yourself is enough to kill most businesses.
—**Jaynie Smith** *Vistage Speaker*

A team that is not accountable, is not a team.
—**Don Schmincke** *Vistage Speaker*

Men have a trick of coming up with what is expected of them, good or bad.
—**Jacob Riis** *Journalist*

One of the greatest challenges we as leaders face is we have very little appreciation why others can't do what we so easily accomplished.
—**Bill Wagner** *Vistage Speaker*

Mistrust a subordinate who never finds fault with his superior.
—**John Churton Collins** *Educator*

If 99% is good enough then gravity will not work for 14 minutes every day.
—**Unknown**

You teach and lead by who you are, sometimes by what you do and seldom by what you say.
—**Russ Walden** *Ridgewood Properties*

You Just Don't Understand...

More is not better, better is better.
—**Howard Hyden**   *Vistage Speaker*

Most customers became inactive after we did.
—**Jim Cecil**   *Vistage Speaker*

Not everyone on the internet is your friend.
—**Mike Foster**   *Vistage Speaker*

If you love your job you haven't worked a day in your life.
—**Tommy Lasorda**   *Baseball Manager*

My business always bores me to death; I prefer other peoples.
—**Oscar Wilde**   *Author*

Good or okay is out of business.
—**Pierre Panos**   *QS America*

Ninety percent of what you do is the same as what the other guy does.
—**Mitch Gooze**   *Vistage Speaker*

No matter how long the runway, a pig still can't fly.
—**Judith Bardwick**   *Author*

Any problem you can make go away with a check is not a problem; it's an expense.
—**Unknown**

No matter what happens, there's somebody who knew it would.
—**Lonny Starr**

No one likes to be sold; everyone likes to buy.
—**Unknown**

If you don't make it, bake it or take it, you support someone who does.
—**Tom Monaghan**   *Domino's*

No plan emerges unscathed from its collision with reality.
—**Herb Meyer** *Vistage Speaker*

Only in a company does deadwood grow roots.
—**Ken Kelly** *Immucor*

No single customer in the history of recorded time has ever said "your price is too high" and meant it.
—**Chuck Reaves** *Vistage Speaker*

Nobody ever forgets where he buried the hatchet.
—**Frank Maguire** *Vistage Speaker*

Leaders without values quickly become leaders without followers.
—**Bill Valentine** *Vistage Speaker*

Whenever you see a successful business, someone once made a courageous decision.
—**Peter Drucker** *Educator*

Not everything that counts can be counted; and not everything that can be counted counts.
—**Albert Einstein** *Physicist*

Old men can't succeed in real estate; they remember how much it used to cost.
—**Unknown**

People who can't let things go are only hoping for a better past.
—**Jay Refinbary** *Vistage Speaker*

Once in a while there's wisdom in recognizing that the boss is.
—**Malcolm Forbes** *Publisher*

Men who complain that the boss is dumb would be out of a job if he were any smarter.
—**Jacob M. Braude** *Humorist*

You Just Don't Understand...

Money is what helps you go to sleep at night; it's not what fires you up to go to work in the morning.
—*Linda Honold*   Vistage Speaker

Opportunity is missed by most people because it is dressed in overalls and looks like work.
—*Thomas Edison*   Inventor

Our lives begin to end the day we become silent upon things that matter.
—*Martin Luther*   Civil Rights Leader

People buy two things: good feelings and problem solutions.
—*Michael LeBoeuf*   Author

People do not quit playing because they grow old. They grow old because they quit playing.
—*Oliver Wendell Holmes*   Jurist

Before you can hit the jackpot, you have to put a coin in the machine.
—*Flip Wilson*   Entertainer

The fewer the facts, the stronger the opinion.
—*Arnold Glasow*   Author

People will put their hearts and souls into a company if they think the owners are putting their hearts and souls into it.
—*Timothy Hendricks*   T.H. Properties

In theory, there is no difference between theory and reality. In reality, there is.
—*Unknown*

Pessimists are usually right and delighted when they're wrong.
—*George Will*   Journalist

Pigs get fat; hogs get slaughtered.
—*Unknown*

Some people are always grumbling because roses have thorns. I'm just thankful that thorns have roses.
—**Alphonse Karr**   *Artist*

Procrastination is opportunity's assassin.
—**Victor Kiam**   *Industrialist*

It's not the questions that get us into trouble, it's the answers.
—**Tom Brokaw**   *Journalist*

Real communication happens when people feel safe.
—**Ken Blanchard**   *Author*

Recession is when a neighbor loses his job. Depression is when you lose yours.
—**Ronald Reagan**   *President*

The only way you can coast is downhill.
—**George Hill**   *PlyMart*

One cannot be a thief in the night and not in the day.
—**Don Schmincke**   *Vistage Speaker*

Remember, you only have to succeed the last time.
—**Brian Tracy**   *Author*

Customer satisfaction surveys are not market research —they're only report cards.
—**Jaynie Smith**   *Vistage Speaker*

The map is not the territory.
—**British Military Commander**

Managing is getting paid for home runs someone else hits.
—**Casey Stengel**   *Baseball Manager*

You Just Don't Understand…

Sales people usually get the biggest paychecks at the end of the month…but they wake up unemployed every day.
—**Reinaldo Niella**   *Del Vieto TV*

The most unfair practice is the equal treatment of unequals.
—**Russ Walden**   *Ridgewood Properties*

Saying "fire" won't burn your mouth; saying "water" won't drown you.
—*Zen Saying*

Seller's remorse is a lot better than buyer's remorse.
—**Lee Mingledorff**   *Mingledorff's*

I would rather have a mind opened by wonder than one closed by belief.
—**Gerry Spence**   *Attorney*

The problem managing long distance equals the square of the distance and the cube of the culture.
—**Unidentified Stanford Economics Professor**

Selling is 90% art and 10% skill. Marketing is 90% skill and 10% art.
—**Charlie Snyder**   *Vistage #150*

The manager asks how and when; the leader asks what and why.
—**Warren Bennis**   *Educator*

Sometimes the majority only means all the fools are on the same side.
—*Unknown*

Sports do not build character. They reveal it.
—**Heywood Broun**   *Commentator*

When a man of money meets a good salesman they usually trade assets.
—**Red Scott**   *Vistage Speaker*

Spring is the time of the year when the ground thaws, trees bud, the income tax falls due - and everyone wins the pennant.
—**Jim Murray**   *Columnist*

Systems run the company, people run the systems.
—**Curt Richardson**   *OtterBox*

The bigger the organization the longer it takes to get a little job done.
—**Unknown**

The faster things change the less you can use facts and the more you need imagination.
—**Stan Davis**   *Consultant*

One of the hardest tasks of leadership is understanding that you are not what you are, but what you're perceived to be by others.
—**Edward L Flom**   *Florida Steel Corp.*

You can observe a lot by just watching.
—**Yogi Berra**   *Baseball Player*

The four most compelling words in business today are 'on time and within budget.'
—**Bud Carter**   *Vistage Chairman*

A little success can create a lot of overhead.
—**Red Scott**   *Vistage Speaker*

The future ain't what it used to be.
—**Yogi Berra**   *Baseball Player*

You Just Don't Understand...

Apathetic people have no complaints or concerns. People who have complaints and concerns have a commitment in the background.
—**Richard Haab** *Vistage Speaker*

The government view of the economy could be summed up in a few short phrases: If it moves, tax it. If it keeps moving, regulate it and if it stops moving, subsidize it.
—**Ronald Reagan** *President*

Nobody wants your product. Nobody wants your service. They only want what your product or service will do for them now.
—**Chuck Reaves** *Vistage Speaker*

The graveyards are filled with indispensable men.
—**Charles De Gaulle** *Political Leader*

No one will ever pay you what your product is worth. They will pay you what they think it is worth.
—**Chuck Reaves** *Vistage Speaker*

The hardest thing to explain is the glaringly evident which everybody has decided not to see.
—**Ayn Rand** *Author*

The headline never says "Passengers crash airplane."
—**Maurice Mascarenhas** *Vistage Speaker*

The little I know I owe to my ignorance.
—**George McGovern** *Governor*

The mindset of a great CEO is 95% psychologist, 4% technologist and 1% being mildly crazy!
—**Hatim Tyabji** *Verifone*

The minute you're satisfied with where you are, you aren't there anymore.
—**Tony Gwynn** *Baseball Player*

Management is about arranging and telling. Leadership is about nurturing and enhancing.
>   —**Tom Peters** **Author**

The most frightening thing in the world is motivated incompetence.
>   —**Richard Dickerson** **Vistage Speaker**

Chances are the biggest problem in your business is you.
>   —**Chris Hanks** *Educator*

The one function that TV News performs very well is that when there is no news, we give it to you with the same emphasis as if it were.
>   —**David Brinkley** *Broadcaster*

Losing feels worse than winning feels good.
>   —**Vin Scully** *Broadcaster*

The one thing that doesn't abide by majority rule is a person's conscience.
>   —**Harper Lee** *Author*

The trouble with the world is that the stupid and the insipid are cocksure and the intelligent are full of doubt.
>   —**Bertrand Russell** *Philosopher*

Good will is another way of saying ego - and it all but disappears in an economic downturn.
>   —**Brian Beaulieu** *Vistage Speaker*

The purpose of the interview is to predict success.
>   —**Barry Shamis** *Vistage Speaker*

People don't want to sell their business; they want it to be bought.
>   —**Peter Collins** *Vistage Speaker*

You Just Don't Understand...

There ain't no future in the past.
    —***Vince Gill*** *Entertainer*

The real problem is not whether machines think but whether men do.
    —***B.F. Skinner*** *Psychologist*

Some people have a habit of scratching things that don't itch.
    —***Unknown***

The reason for the divorce was present on the first date.
    —***Pat Murray*** *Vistage Speaker*

The salesman who can't articulately present your product's value proposition, ultimately resorts to discounting to get deals.
    —***Gil Cargill*** *Vistage Speaker*

Too often, hiring is a process frequently conducted by people with only a tenuous grasp of the work the candidate is being considered for.
    —***Tom Peters*** *Author*

The sexual revolution is over and the microbes won.
    —***P.J. O'Rourke*** *Humorist*

The starting point of all achievement is desire...Weak desire brings weak results; just a small amount of fire brings a small amount of heat.
    —***Napoleon Hill*** *Author*

People who are born round don't die square.
    —***Cus D'Amato*** *Boxing trainer*

The soft stuff is the hard stuff.
    —***Richard Leider,*** *Author*

Money is like manure, you spread it around it does a lot of good. If you stack it up in one place, it stinks like hell.
  —*Clint Murchison*   Industrialist

The worst thing you can ever hear from a client is 'I didn't know you did that.'
  —*Richard Kopelman*   Habif, Arogeti & Wynne

As a leader you're probably not doing a good job unless your employees can do a good impression of you when you're not around.
  —*Patrick Lencioni*   The Table Group

A candle loses nothing by lighting another candle.
  —*Unknown*
There are no business problems; there are only personal problems that manifest in a business setting.
  —*Morrie Shechtman*   Vistage Speaker

If you are too scared to go to the brink, you are lost.
  —*John Foster Dulles*   Secretary of State

There is always an easy solution to every human problem: neat, plausible and wrong.
  —*Henry Louis Mencken*   Humorist

Low performers see feedback as an attack on their ego.
  —*Harvey Goldberg*   Vistage Speaker

There is as much risk in doing nothing as in doing something.
  —*Trammel Crow*   Developer

A salesman without enthusiasm is just a clerk.
  —*Harry F. Banks*   Author

If they put a muskrat where the rabbit is the greyhound won't run.
  —*Scott Seydel*   The Seydel Company

You Just Don't Understand...

If you're doing business today the way you were doing business five years ago, you're on your way out of business.
—**Frank Maguire** *Vistage Speaker*

There is no point in doing well that which you should not be doing at all.
—**Thomas K. Connellan** *Author*

When the need is great enough, the expertise great enough, price is not a factor.
—**Max Carey** *Vistage Speaker*

There is no such thing as bad weather, just inappropriate clothing.
—**Karen Meenan** *Vistage Chairman*

There's a fine line between chaos and creation.
—**Paul McCartney** *Musician*

Things break even for all of us. For example, we all get the same amount of ice. The rich get it in the summertime and the poor get it in the winter.
—**Bat Masterson** *Lawman*

Well behaved women rarely make history.
—**Laurel Thatcher Ulrich** *Author*

Think carefully before you send ducks to eagle's school.
—**Bob Weaver** *Vistage Speaker*

We make a living by what we get, but we make a life by what we give.
—**Winston Churchill** *Government Leader*

Those who suppress freedom always do so in the name of law and order.
—**John V. Lindsay** *Mayor*

You must learn from the mistakes of others. You can't possibly live long enough to make them all yourself.
—**Sam Levenson** *Comedian*

Too many people are thinking of security instead of opportunity. They seem more afraid of life than death.
—**James F. Byrnes** *Congressman*

Well timed silence hath more eloquence than speech.
—**M.T. Tupper**

We insist that all our employees contribute their minds.
—**Akio Morita** *Sony*

Management is a function, it is not a class.
—**Catherine Meek** *Vistage Speaker*

Though familiarity may not breed contempt it takes the edge off admiration.
—**William Hazlitt** *Economist*

Time is more valuable than money. You can get more money, but you cannot get more time.
—**Jim Rohn** *Author*

Your job as a CEO is not to solve problems every day - it is to seize opportunities. To work on the business instead of in it.
—**Michael Gerber** *Author*

Too many people are down on whatever they're not up on.
—**Allen Soden** *Half Full Group*

When you tell a story try to have a point. It makes it so much more interesting to the listener.
—**Steve Martin** *Entertainer*

Too much of a good thing is wonderful.
—**Mae West** *Entertainer*

You Just Don't Understand…

There's a funny thing about customers: It's OK to make them mad…just don't piss them off.
—**Clark Johnson**   *Vistage Speaker*

We abuse our employees and pass the savings on to you.
—**Dilbert**   *Cartoon Character*

There are two ways to slide easily through life: to believe everything and to doubt everything. Both ways save thinking.
—**Alfred Korzybski**   *Philosopher*

We probably wouldn't worry about what people think about us if we knew how seldom they do.
—**Roseanne Barr**   *Entertainer*

There are three kinds of companies today: Those who make things happen… Those who watch things happen… Those who wonder what has happened.
—**Peter Drucker**   *Educator*

We're all on this spaceship Earth together and there are no passengers; everyone is crew.
—**Buckminster Fuller**   *Inventor*

The most important role for the CEO is to be the CPO - the Chief Priority Officer.
—**Bob Thomson**   *Vistage Speaker*

When a lion lays down with a lamb, the lamb doesn't get much sleep.
—**Woody Allen**   *Entertainer*

The most successful businessman is the man who holds onto the old just as long as it is good and grabs the new just as soon as it is better.
—**Robert P. Vanderpoel**   *Editor*

When you get to the top, don't forget to send the elevator back down.
> **—Forbes Magazine**

There are no persons capable of stooping so low as those who desire to rise in the world.
> **—Lady Maguerite Blessington** *Author*

Whether you believe you can or you can't, you are right.
> **—Henry Ford** *Industrialist*

The boss' secretary can wield great power, like the king's mistress, without any authority at all.
> **—Unknown**

Winners have simply formed the habit of doing things losers don't like to do.
> **—Albert E.N. Gray** *Author*

The biggest enemy to increased quality and productivity is multi tasking.
> **—Eli Goldratt** *Consultant*

Without data, you're just another schmuck with an opinion.
> **—Chris Anderson** *Vistage Speaker*

The only thing riveting about bookkeeping is that it's the only word in the English language with three double letters in a row - and nothing else.
> **—Nick Setchell** *Vistage Speaker*

Work is accomplished by those employees who have not yet reached their level of incompetence.
> **—Laurence J. Peter** *Educator*

Work should be more fun than fun.
> **—Noel Coward** *Author*

You Just Don't Understand...

Yesterday is ashes; tomorrow wood. Only today does the fire burn brightly.
  —***Eskimo Proverb***

If it doesn't absorb you, if it isn't any fun, don't do it.
  —***D.H. Lawrence*** *Author*

Your most unhappy customers are your greatest source of learning.
  —***Bill Gates*** *Microsoft*

Enjoy yourself. These are "the good old days" you're going to miss years ahead.
  —***Unknown***

If you ain't got a hernia yet, you ain't pulling your share of the load.
  —***George Steinbrenner*** *Industrialist*

You can't create a general by asking privates to volunteer.
  —***Michael Price*** *CEO Ventures*

You've got to do your own growing no matter how tall your grandfather was.
  —***Irish Proverb***

The essence of leadership is not to manage and change others. It is to manage and change yourself.
  —***Ned Hamson*** *Editor*

Young people today don't fear change; it's all they have ever known.
  —***Marc Muchnick*** *Vistage Speaker*

Your chances of success are directly proportional to the degree of pleasure you derive from what you do.
  —***Michael Korda*** *Author*

53

There is no greater joy, nor greater reward, than to make a fundamental difference in someone's life.
—*Sister Mary Rose McGeady*   *Child Advocate*

If everyone is thinking alike then someone isn't thinking.
—*Gen. George Patton*   *Military Leader*

Your job is to make what you do obsolete before your competition does it for you.
—*J. Howard Shelov*   *Vistage Speaker*

If you place a small value on yourself, rest assured that the world will not raise the price.
—*Unknown*

Every customer we have knows a customer we could have.
—*Chuck Reaves*   *Vistage Speaker*

"Knowing" is one of the most dangerous places you can be, "assuming" is even worse.
—*Kraig Kramers*   *Vistage Speaker*

The Unfair Advantage

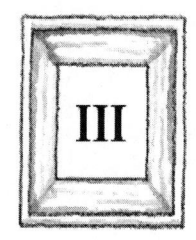

III

Every viable product or service has
an "unfair advantage" over its competition.
What's yours? How are you leveraging it?

The Unfair Advantage...

Those who bring sunshine to the lives of others cannot keep it from themselves.
—***Irish Blessing***

Better culture, better performance, better bottom line.
—***Andy Fleming*** *Vistage Speaker*

Customers will go out of their way to buy a superior product...and you can charge them a toll for the trip.
—***Frank Perdue*** *Perdue Poultry*

A fine quotation is a diamond on the finger of a man of wit, and a pebble in the hand of a fool.
—***Joseph Roux*** *Cartographer*

Decide like a Democracy; implement like a dictatorship.
—***Peter Schutz*** *Vistage Speaker*

A smart businessman makes money in his own business and knows better than to lose it in somebody else's.
—***Ron Rowe*** *Vistage Speaker*

Demographics win - always.
—***Herb Meyer*** *Vistage Speaker*

Advertising is one of the few callings in which it is advisable to pay attention to someone else's business.
—***Henry Ford*** *Industrialist*

An individual without information cannot take responsibility; an individual who is given information cannot help but take responsibility.
—***Jan Carlzon*** *Scandinavian Airlines*

An investment in knowledge pays the best interest.
—***Benjamin Franklin*** *Inventor*

Be fearful when others are greedy and greedy when others are fearful.
—**Warren Buffet**   *Industrialist*

Blessed are the flexible, for they shall not be bent out of shape.
—**Michael McGriff**   *Author*

Budget for training just as you do for your utilities. You can't shut either off.
—**Bob Desatnick**   *Vistage Speaker*

Concessions the other party doesn't see have no value to you.
—**Jack Kaine**   *Vistage Speaker*

Consider the usefulness of the postage stamp; its usefulness consists in the ability to stick to one thing until it gets there.
—**Josh Billings**   *Humorist*

Customers, when given a choice of where they spend their money will invariably go back to that place where they have been made to feel special.
—**Marshall Fields**   *Businessman*

Discipline is the training that makes punishment unnecessary.
—**Robert E. Lee**   *Military Leader*

Emotion commits your customer to your brand; not facts; not logic; emotion.
—**Don Rheem**   *Vistage Speaker*

Entrepreneurs don't need degrees like lawyers and doctors do. They are credentialed by virtue of their track record.
—**Fred Wilson**   *Union Square Ventures*

The Unfair Advantage...

Ethics must begin at the top of an organization. It is a leadership issue and the chief executive must set the example.
—**Edward Hennessy** *Allied Signal*

Sheep led by a lion would defeat lions led by a sheep.
— **Arabian Proverb**

I have never been hurt by anything I didn't say.
—**Calvin Coolidge** *President*

I have 1,000 friends I have yet to meet.
—**Bob Cleveland** *Caterpillar*

Everyone who stops learning is old, whether at 20 or 80. Anyone who keeps learning stays young. The greatest thing in life is to keep your mind young.
—**Henry Ford** *Industrialist*

Everyone who's ever taken a shower has an idea. It's the person who gets out of the shower, dries off and does something about it that makes a difference.
—**Nolan Bushnell** *Atari*

Focused action beats intellectual brilliance every time in the marketplace of human affairs.
—**Mark Sanborn** *Author*

For 25 years you've paid only for my hands when you could have had my brain for free.
—**Retiring GM worker**

Giving people a little more than they expect is a good way to get back a lot more than you'd expect.
—**Robert Half** *Author*

You can get a lot more done with a staff of 14 who care than with 25 or 30 who don't.
—**Brian Laoruangroch.** *Green Mobile*

Great businesses, whether they're Starbucks or Home Depot or McDonald's, create fans; fans who buy into the model and then reinforce the brand.
—**Vernon Hill**   Commerce Bancorp

Great leaders are approachable people with a low tolerance for poor performance.
—**Dan Wertenberg**   Vistage Speaker

Great work places are defined less by wages and working conditions as by feelings, attitudes and relationships.
—**Frank Maguire**   Vistage Speaker

Harley Davidson has created a cult and they sell memberships - it ain't about motorcycles.
—**Peter Schutz**   Vistage Speaker

How old would you be if you didn't know how old you was?
—**Satchel Paige**   Baseball Player

I have never hit a golf ball without first seeing it go into the hole.
—**Jack Nicklaus**   Golfer

I prefer rogues to imbeciles, because they sometimes take a rest.
—**Alexander Dumas**   Author

If my competitors were drowning, I'd put a fire hose in their mouth.
—**Ray Kroc**   McDonalds

If we look at our people as Super Stars they will do whatever is necessary to validate our perception.
—**Ron Rowe**   Vistage Speaker

The Unfair Advantage...

Where there's mystery, there's margin.
—**Gerry Layo** *Vistage Speaker*

If you can't make decisions and build relationships, you won't have a job in the future.
—**Morrie Shechtman** *Vistage Speaker*

If you spend a lot of time figuring out who you're going to hire you'll have to spend far less time figuring out who to fire.
—**Michael Lotito** *Vistage Speaker*

If you think education is expensive, try ignorance.
—**Derek Bok** *Harvard University*

If you want to be Superman you've got to learn to fly in bad weather.
—**Michael Canic** *Vistage Speaker*

Imagination is more important than knowledge.
—**Albert Einstein** *Physicist*

Money will always flow towards opportunity, and there is an abundance of that in America. Our best days lie ahead.
—**Warren Buffet** *Industrialist*

In a negotiation the dumbest question you don't ask is the one you don't ask.
—**Jack Kaine** *Vistage Speaker*

In a time of drastic change it is the learner who will inherit the future.
—**Eric Hoffer** *Philosopher*

In an uneven economy there is always a flight to safety.
—**Dean Minuto** *Vistage Speaker*

In business the competition will bite you if you keep running; if you stand still, they will swallow you.
—**William S. Knudsen** *Industrialist*

In negotiations, dumb is smart and smart is dumb.
—*Jack Kaine*   *Vistage Speaker*

In school it's called copying, plagiarizing - it's bad; in business we call it "best practices."
—*Gary Markle*   *Vistage Speaker*

In the beginner's mind there are many possibilities. In the mind of the expert there are few.
—*D.T. Suzuki*   *Philosopher*

It is always better to leave the party early.
—*Bill Watterson*   *Cartoonist*

It is at the point of break downs that we have break through.
—*Bill Schwarz*   *Vistage Speaker*

It's more important to hire people with the right qualities than with the right experience.
—*J.W. Marriott*   *Marriott Hotels*

It's always good when followers believe in their leaders, but it's even better when leaders believe in their followers.
—*Dr. Mardy Grothe*   *Vistage Speaker*

It's better to have a company bound by love than one motivated by fear.
—*Herb Kelleher*   *Southwest Airlines*

It's better to know the judge than the law.
—*Boss Tweed*   *Political Leader*

Judge a man by his questions rather than his answers.
—*Voltaire*   *Philosopher*

Leaders are made by the people who follow.
—*Red Scott*   *Vistage Speaker*

Leadership and learning are indispensable to each other.
   —***John F. Kennedy*** *President*

Learning is the only sustainable source of competitive advantage.
   —***Karl Hellman*** *Vistage Speaker*

Make sure that bad news travels quickly to those who can do something about it.
   —***Michael LeBoeuf*** *Author*

Marketing isn't a department in your company; it's what your company does.
   —***Steve Yastrow*** *Vistage Speaker*

Nothing gives one person so much advantage over another as to remain cool and unruffled under all circumstances.
   —***Thomas Jefferson*** *President*

Most of us know how to get all the way to second place.
   —***Tom Searcy*** *Vistage Speaker*

Rise early. Work late. Strike oil.
   —***J. Paul Getty*** *Industrialist*

Most people are much better at waiting to speak than listening.
   —***Steve Wiley*** *Vistage Speaker*

Most people stay mediocre to protect against loss.
   —***Morrie Shechtman*** *Vistage Speaker*

My first message is: Listen; listen, listen to the people who do the work.
   —***H. Ross Perot*** *Industrialist*

Never create demand for your product. Create it for your brand.
—*Max Carey*   Vistage Speaker

No man ever listened himself out of a job.
—*Calvin Coolidge*   President

Nothing is better than having a bunch of partners working to make you rich.
—*Donald Luger*   Lockwood Greene

Nothing is really work unless you would rather be doing something else.
—*James M. Barrie*   Author

Permitting colleagues to participate in decision making is not so much a favor to the participants as it is to the executive.
—*Prof. Ray E. Brown*   Educator

We're so focused on our company's mission that we could pee through a straw.
—*Richard Tait*   Cranium

One machine can do the work of 50 ordinary people. No machine can do the work of an extraordinary person.
—*Unknown*

Passion for who you are and what you do will carry you a lot further than just knowledge!
—*Bob Dabic*   Vistage Chairman

Passion persuades.
—*Anita Roddick*   The Body Shop

People are the only sustainable advantage of an organization.
—*Richard Teerlink*   Harley-Davidson

The Unfair Advantage...

People can't see it your way until you first see it their way.
—*Jack Kaine*   Vistage Speaker

People do not resist their own ideas.
—*Deanna Berg*   Vistage Speaker

People don't quit jobs they love.
—*Malcolm Moore*   Vistage Speaker

People remember people who remember them.
—*Marshall Fields*   Businessman

People who know 'how' always work for people who know 'why'.
—*Charles Bernard*   Vistage Speaker

Perfection will be tolerated.
—*Bob McWhirter*   Federal Express & Continental Airlines

Perpetual optimism is a force multiplier.
—*Gen. Colin Powell*   Secretary of State

Practice doesn't make perfect; practice makes permanent.
—*Amy K Hutchens*   Vistage Speaker

Price tells the customer the quality of the product or the integrity of the transaction.
—*Chuck Reaves*   Vistage Speaker

Profit is the applause you get from appreciative customers and committed employees.
—*Ken Blanchard*   Author

Reform always comes from below. No man with four aces ever asks for a new deal.
—*Unknown*

Russia failed because centralized planning cannot work in an information age.
—*Harry Dent*   *Vistage Speaker*

People who trust each other don't sue each other.
—*Donald Phinn*   *Vistage Speaker*

Salesman should sell; everyone else should do everything else.
—*Gil Cargill*   *Vistage Speaker*

Service is to take care of the customer the way that the customer wants to be taken care of.
—*Horst Schulze*   *Ritz Carlton*

Silence is a great weapon in negotiations.
—*Charles Ackerman*   *Ackerman Real Estate*

Some people won't negotiate until they know you're ready to litigate.
—*Jack Kaine*   *Vistage Speaker*

No executive has ever suffered because his subordinates were strong and effective.
—*Peter Drucker*   *Educator*

Test fast, fail fast, adjust fast.
—*Tom Peters*   *Author*

Some persons are likeable in spite of their unswerving integrity.
—*Don Marquis*   *Journalist*

Stay opportunity focused. One opportunity can change the course of a business, while solving all the problems just gets you back to zero.
—*Fred Chaney*   *Vistage Chairman*

Strategy is finding a niche and building barriers. Nothing more.
   —***Jerry Goldress*** *Vistage Speaker*

Strategy without tactics is the slowest route to victory. Tactics without strategy is the noise before defeat.
   —***Sun Tzu*** *Philosopher*

Success is going from failure to failure without loss of enthusiasm.
   —***Winston Churchill*** *Government Leader*

Success seems to be connected with action. Successful men keep moving. They make mistakes, but they don't quit.
   —***Conrad Hilton*** *Hilton Hotels*

Superior performance is a common trait among uncommon people.
   —***Unknown***

The answer is in the room.
   —***John Marcus*** *Vistage Member St. Louis*

The art and science of asking questions is the source of all knowledge.
   —***Thomas Berger*** *Author*

The best of all leaders is the one who helps people so that eventually they don't need him.
   —***Lao Tzu*** *Philosopher*

The best time to sell a business is when it has no place to go but up.
   —***Jerry Goldress*** *Vistage Speaker*

The closer you get the reward to the behavior, the more you influence the behavior.
   —***Ron Fleisher*** *Vistage Speaker*

The human mind, once stretched to a new idea, never goes back to its original dimension.
—*Oliver Wendell Holmes*   Jurist

The important thing is to win at the slowest speed possible.
—*Johnny Rutherford*   Race Car Driver

The longer a prospect waits to buy the less competition there is for the business.
—*Jim Cecil*   Vistage Speaker

The manager will climb the ladder. The leader makes sure it's against the right wall.
—*Stanley Hynes*   Businessman

The most important business you do is the business you don't do.
—*Tom Searcy*   Vistage Speaker

The most important principle about openness is that everyone is invited to join.
—*Eric Schmidt*   Google

The most important thing you can give your people is your time.
—*Larry King*   Vistage Speaker

The most significant resource available to us in these times are our employees' ideas.
—*Jeff Peterson*   Vistage Speaker

The only power, the only tool, leverage, you have as a leader, is your example.
—*Pat Murray*   Vistage Speaker

The only real difference between one organization and another is the performance of its people.
—*Peter Drucker*   Educator

The Unfair Advantage…

The only sustainable competitive advantage is your people.
   —**Barry Shamis**   *Vistage Speaker*

The pampered customer is the retained customer.
   —**Jim Cecil**   *Vistage Speaker*

The prize goes to the person who sees the future the quickest.
   —**William Stiritz**   *Ralston Purina*

The real company values, as opposed to nice sounding values, are shown by who gets recognized, promoted or let go.
   —**Reed Hastings**   *Netflix*

The most compelling reason to populate your company with "A players" is to be sure you can deliver on your service promise.
   —**Ann Rhoades,** *Vistage Speaker*

You don't have to be sick to get better.
   —**James Newton**   *Vistage Speaker*

The root source of all competitive advantage is an organization's relative ability to learn faster than its competition.
   — **Hayward Daily Review**

The trouble with being punctual is that nobody's there to appreciate it.
   —**Irving S. Cobb**   *Humorist*

The war today is more for your employees than for your customers. If they get your employees they get your customers.
   —**Bud Mingledorff**   *Mingledorff's*

The way to succeed is to double your failure rate.
   —**Thomas Watson**   *IBM*

The will to succeed is important but what's more important is the will to prepare.
—**Bobby Knight**   *Basketball Coach*

There is no talent shortage if you're a great place to work.
—**Tom Peters**   *Author*

There is something that is much more scarce, something that is rarer than ability. It is the ability to recognize ability.
—**Elbert Hubbard**   *Author*

Those who make the worst use of their time are the first to complain of its brevity.
—**Jean De Labruyere**

Trust comes from keeping a series of small commitments.
—**Deanna Berg**   *Vistage Speaker*

We all know what to do, few of us do.
—**Bob Sutton**   *Author*

We do not see things as they are; we see things as we are.
—**The Talmud**

We're drowning in information but starved for knowledge.
—**Unknown**

What we need is less process and more passion.
—**Frank Maguire**   *Vistage Speaker*

When customers leave for greener pastures they usually give price as the reason when in fact it's often simple neglect.
—**John R. Graham**   *Author*

The Unfair Advantage…

When too much emphasis is placed on job definition, one is apt to think more about the limits of authority than upon opportunities.
—**Clarence Francis** *General Foods*

When we shorten the time cycle we reduce errors and cost and increase customer satisfaction.
—**Michael Sonduck** *Vistage Speaker*

When you're better than "good enough" your price is too high.
—**Sam Bowers** *Vistage Speaker*

When you're looking at truth versus gossip, truth doesn't stand a chance.
—**Barbara Mikkelson** *Snopes.com*

With money, you are wise, and you are handsome, and you sing well too.
—**Yiddish Proverb**

You can be young without money but you can't be old without it.
—**Tennessee Williams** *Author*

You can't train for once and for all, any more than you can eat, for once and for all.
—**James Newton** *Vistage Speaker*

Your attitude controls your destiny - in business as well as in health.
—**Dr. Jerry Kornfield** *Vistage Speaker*

You don't convince people by telling them; you convince people by asking them.
— **Zig Ziglar** *Trainer*

You have to go to college to get a high school education.
—**Michael Milken** *Industrialist*

You'll never have all the information you need to make a decision. If you did, it would be a foregone conclusion, not a decision.
—***Unknown***

You'll pay a little more, wait a little longer, in order to do business with people you like.
—**Ron Arden**   *Vistage Speaker*

Your business will never be easier than it is today.
—**Michael Basch**   *Vistage Speaker*

Your customers don't care how much you know until they know how much you care.
—***Unknown***

You can't achieve anything without getting in someone's way. You can't be both detached and effective.
—**Abba Eban**   *Prime Minister*

In Search Of The Magic Bullet

IV

'The tough answer is that there are no easy answers. There are no magic bullets.

In Search Of The Magic Bullet...

A barking dog is often more useful than a sleeping lion.
   —**Arabian Proverb**

We are drowning in data and starving for information.
   —**John Nesbit** *Educator*

A certain amount of opposition is a great help; kites rise against, not with the wind.
   —**John Neal** *Author*

A decision is an action an executive must take when he has information so incomplete that the answer does not suggest itself.
   —**Arthur William Bradford**

A fanatic is someone who redoubles his efforts after he's lost sight of the goal.
   —**Lauch McKinnon** *RockBridge Commercial Bank*

All cats are gray in the dark
   —**Benjamin Franklin** *Inventor*

A key driver for relationships, revenue and results, is simplicity.
   —**Jeff Blackman** *Vistage Speaker*

A leader takes people where they want to go. A great leader takes people where they don't necessarily want to go but ought to be.
   —**Rosalynn Carter** *President's Wife*

A man can succeed at almost anything for which he has unlimited enthusiasm.
   —**Charles Schwab** *Schwab Company*

Business is 50% about product - the other 90% as Yogi would figure it, is the people.
   —**Peter Schutz** *Vistage Speaker*

A professional is someone who can do his best work when he doesn't feel like it.
—**Alistair Cooke** *Media Personality*

A prudent person profits from personal experience, a wise one from the experience of others.
—**Dr. Joseph Colins**

Genius begins great works, labor alone finishes them.
—**Joseph Joubert** *Author*

Action speaks louder than words - but nearly as often.
—**Unknown**

Almost all big mistakes are made when people perceive things are going well.
—**Jason Beans** *Rising Medical Solutions Inc.*

An angry customer can be one of your company's biggest assets.
—**Howard Hyden** *Vistage Speaker*

Another flaw in the human character is that everybody wants to build and nobody wants to do maintenance.
—**Kurt Vonnegut** *Author*

The first responsibility of a leader is to define reality, the last is to say "Thank you." In between the two, the leader must become a servant.
Herman DePree *Herman Miller*

Be the parents of our future, not the offspring of our past.
—**David Houle** *Vistage Speaker*

Being listened to feels so much like being loved we can't tell the difference.
— **David Ogilvie** *Advertising Executive*

In Search Of The Magic Bullet...

Beside the noble art of getting things done, there is the noble art of leaving things undone. The wisdom of life consists in the elimination of non-essentials.
—**Lin Yutang**   *Author*

A mistake happens only once; underperformance is a pattern.
—**Greg Bustin**   *Vistage Speaker*

Businesses that are cash machines don't have those licenses in perpetuity.
—**Garry Fehrman**   *Tensar*

Certain positions in your company are career positions - not career paths.
—**Kraig Kramers**   *Vistage Speaker*

Changing compensation means changing the culture of your company and there needs to be trust to do that.
—**Catherine Meek**   *Vistage Speaker*

Character is the discipline to follow through after the emotion of making the decision has passed.
—**Hiram Smith**   *Franklin Planner*

Closing the sale is not an event; it is just part of the process.
—**Chuck Reaves**   *Vistage Speaker*

Collections is TQM from the back of the parade.
—**Abe Sanchez**   *Vistage Speaker*

Computers make very fast, very accurate mistakes.
—**Unknown**

Confused minds say "no."
—**Mike Ruland**   *Peachtree Residential*

Curiosity is life. Assumption is death. Look around. Be a sponge.
—**Mike Parker** *Nike*

Diversification may mean higher sales but it also usually means lower profits.
—**Mitch Gooze** *Vistage Speaker*

Don't tell them anything about what you do until you've learned everything about what they do.
—**David Yoho** *Vistage Speaker*

We become what we tolerate; we encourage what we allow.
—**Mike Richardson** *Vistage Speaker*

High earners can appreciate a small reward if it is unexpected. Even billionaires appreciate a Christmas sweater from their Mom.
—**Eric Mosley** *Globoforce*

Be the change you want to see.
—**Mahatma Gandhi** *Government Leader*

Don't try to explain it. Just sell it.
—**Col. Tom Parker** *Personal Manager*

Change is good; you go first.
—**Dilbert** *Cartoon Character*

Don't let your high performers down by keeping the dead wood around.
—**Al Duncan** *Thomas E. Strauss Inc.*

New? New is easy, Right is hard.
—**Craig Federighi** *Apple*

Eagles don't flock - you have to find them one at a time.
—**H. Ross Perot** *Industrialist*

In Search Of The Magic Bullet…

Every growth opportunity I've had in business has been constrained, not by capital, but by people.
—**Malcolm Moore** *Vistage Speaker*

Everybody gets so much information all day long that they lose their common sense.
—**Gertrude Stein** *Author*

People in distress will sometimes prefer a problem that is familiar to a solution that in not.
—**Neil Postman** *Author*

Everything should be made as simple as possible and no simpler.
—**Albert Einstein** *Physicist*

Financial security is everything it's cracked up to be - but it is not happiness and it's not health.
—**Walt Sutton** *Vistage Speaker*

Forget past mistakes. Forget failures. Forget everything except what you're going to do now and do it.
—**William Durant** *Founder General Motors*

If you give it away, you can sell a lot more.
—**Brad Fallon** *Vistage Speaker*

How do you run a great company today? It must be professionally managed and entrepreneurially driven.
—**Jerry Goldress** *Vistage Speaker*

I am a man of fixed and unbending principles, the first of which is to be flexible at all times.
—**Everett Dirksen** *Senator*

It's difficult to talk about the rules if you're already playing the game.
—**Richard Palmer** *Vistage Speaker*

I can think of nothing less pleasurable than a life devoted to pleasure.
—**John D. Rockefeller Sr.**   *Standard Oil*

I run a hot dog stand. We put mustard on it and shove it out the door. If you want catsup go somewhere else.
—**Dave Wise**   *Wise Business Forms*

I want to arrive home from work (mentally and emotionally) at the same time my body does!
—**Tim Wilkinson**   *SELCO/ECC*

There is no such thing as insufficient resources, only insufficient resourcefulness,
—**Tony Hseih**   *Zappos*

I'd rather go down in flames than never to have flown.
—**Russ Walden**   *Ridgewood Properties*
Ideas are a commodity. Execution of them is not.
—**Michael Dell**   *Dell Computers*

If all we allow our customers to bring to the table is their money then all they will think about is our price.
—**Bruce Dell**   *Lockwood Greene*

If analysts were any good at business they would be rich men instead of advisers to rich men.
—**Kirk Kerkorian**   *Industrialist*

If at first the idea is not absurd, then there is no hope for it.
—**Albert Einstein**   *Physicist*

If we aren't customer driven, our cars won't be either.
— **Donald Peterson**   *Ford Motor Co*

Parents, who seek to protect their children from disappointment, create pessimists.
—**Steven Snyder**   *Vistage Speaker*

In Search Of The Magic Bullet…

If you can raise your level of customer service to mediocre, you will stand out in the crowd.
—**Tom Peters** *Author*

If you can trust a man, a written contract is a waste of paper. If you cannot trust a man, a written contract is still a waste of paper.
—**J. Paul Getty** *Industrialist*

If we knew what we were doing, it wouldn't be called research.
—**Albert Einstein** *Physicist*

If you don't give corrective feedback you rob the individual of the chance to improve.
—**Maurice Mascarenhas** *Vistage Speaker*

If you have an opportunity to grow your company and you really believe in it, the capital will follow you.
—**Gordon Tunstall** *Vistage Speaker*

If you want to be the biggest, you have to be the best first.
—**Jim Lientz** *Bank of America*

If you listen closely enough your customers will explain your business to you.
—**Peter Schutz** *Vistage Speaker*

If you measure solely on the basis of sales, you'll never know if you customers are buying better than your salesman are selling.
—**Gil Cargill** *Vistage Speaker*

If you really want to be successful in life, don't blur the edges.
—**Dr. Michael Johnson** *Author*

In business, you need workers who are well trained, and managers who are well educated.
—**Roger Blackwell** *Vestige Speaker*

If you wait for the robins, spring will be over.
—**Warren Buffet** *Industrialist*

If you want to free yourself enormously as an individual you give up all thought of entitlement. Nobody owes you anything. Everything has to be created.
—**Dan Sullivan** *Author*

If you want total security go to prison. There you're fed, clothed, given medical care, and so on. The only thing lacking is freedom.
—**Gen. Dwight D. Eisenhower** *President*

If you're not having fun there's no passion. If there's no passion there can be no success.
—**Peter Schutz** *Vistage Speaker*

If you're going to hitch your wagon to a star, you better make sure it's a rising star.
—**Charles Smithgall III** *Aaron's*

I'm almost paralyzed by my inability to see things in black and white.
—**Tina Fey** *Comedienne*

Improve by 1% a day, and in 70 days you're twice as good.
—**Alan Weiss** *Author*

In the business world everyone is paid in two coins: cash and experience. Take the experience first; the cash will come later.
—**Harold Green** *ITT*

In Search Of The Magic Bullet...

In times of rapid change experience may be your own worst enemy.
—**J. Paul Getty**   *Industrialist*

It is difficult to achieve success in business through Super Stars.
—**Peter Schutz**   *Vistage Speaker*

It is easier to fight for one's principles than to live up to them.
—**Alfred Adler**   *Psychologist*

It is never too late to learn, but sometimes it's too early.
—**Charlie Brown**   *Cartoon Character*

It's almost cheaper to file a lawsuit than to buy a lottery ticket - and the chances of a payoff are greater.
—**Phillip Van Hooser**   *Vistage Speaker*

It's better to opt for passing brilliance rather than permanent mediocrity.
—**Ed Ryan**   *Vistage Speaker*

It's easier to build boys and girls than to mend men and women.
—**Truett Cathy**   *Chick-Fil-A*

You've got to be in business to be in business.
—**David Borreson**   *Peachtree Residential*

It's not the process you utilize but the passion you possess that will make the difference.
—**Frank Maguire**   *Vistage Speaker*

It's not the strongest of the species that survive or the most intelligent, but the one most responsive to change.
—**Charles Darwin**   *Scientist*

It's what you learn after you know it all that counts.
—*John Wooden* *Basketball Coach*

It's better to have some of the questions than all of the answers.
—*James Thurber* *Humorist*

Leadership is confusing as hell.
—*Tom Peters* *Author*

It's easier to see eye-to-eye when you're face-to-face.
—*Kemmons Wilson* *Holiday Inn*

Knowing is the enemy of learning.
—*Larry Wilson* *Vistage Speaker*

Leadership is about taking the organization to a place it would not have otherwise gone without you in a value-adding measurable way.
—*George M.C. Fisher* *Eastman Kodak*

Leadership is simple - it's just not easy.
—*Phillip Van Hooser* *Vistage Speaker*

Let's not confuse activity with progress.
—*Paul Bortree*

Life will hold some perfect days for you in the coming year. Make sure you are available.
—*Barbara Pagano* *Vistage Speaker*

Lord, please grant me all my desires as you forgive me for asking.
—*David Hanson* *SyncroFlo*

Marketing's job is to think like your customer.
—*Mitch Gooze* *Vistage Speaker*

Mere change is not growth. Growth is the synthesis of change and continuity, and where there is no continuity there is no growth.
—**C.S. Lewis** *Author*

Be distinct or be extinct.
—**Tom Peters** *Author*

Money follows good deals, products and services.
—**Gordon Tunstall** *Vistage Speaker*

Money spent on employee recognition has ten times the impact as that provided for compensation.
—**Kraig Kramers** *Vistage Speaker*

More people would learn from their mistakes if they weren't so busy denying them.
—**Unknown**

Most companies that go bankrupt do so during an upturn in the economy…they don't have and can't get the working capital necessary to complete.
—**Brian Beaulieu** *Vistage Speaker*

Most of the problems you have are yesterday's solution.
—**Bill Schwarz** *Vistage Speaker*

Much good work is lost for the lack of a little more.
—**Edward H. Harriman** *Railroad Tycoon*

You gain an edge by understanding your customer's customers before your customers do.
—**Roger Blackwell** *Vistage Speaker*

Never forget that only dead fish swim with the stream.
—**Malcom Muggeridge** *Author*

People are the common denominator of progress…no improvement is possible with unimproved people.
—**John Kenneth Galbraith** *Economist*

Never have a strategic partner with values different from yours.
—**Jerry Goldress** *Vistage Speaker*

Never let the urgent crowd out the important.
—**Stephen R. Covey** *Author*

The quality of listening has an impact on the quality of service. Firms intent on improving service need to listen continuously.
—**Leonard Berry, A. Parasuraman,** *Sloan Business Review*

Never mistake activity for achievement.
—**John Wooden** *Basketball Coach*

Nine of 10 small businesses spend their profits on their areas of weakness instead of the things that make them money.
—**Gideon Malherbe** *Vistage Speaker*

No one has a budget for cutting costs.
—**David Taylor-Klaus** *Digital Positions*

Not doing more than the average is what keeps the average down.
—**Unknown**

Nothing is more dangerous than an idea when it is the only one you have.
—**Emile Chartier** *Philospher*

One of the facts may be that you don't have all the facts.
—**Livia Whisenhunt** *PS Energy*

People who enjoy what they are doing invariably do it well.
—**Joe Gibbs,** *Football Coach*

In Search Of The Magic Bullet…

One person with passion is better than fourty people merely interested.
   —**E.M. Foster** *Author*

Only a fool tests the water with both feet.
   —**African Proverb**

People choose problems they can't solve over solutions they don't like.
   —**Lee Thayer** *Vistage Speaker*

People do business with people, not with corporate logos.
   —**Skip Horn** *Bank of Hiawassee*

People don't choose their careers; they are engulfed by them.
   —**John Dos Passos** *Author*

Sunlight is the best disinfectant.
   —**Louis Brandeis** *US Supreme Court*

People invest in who you are and what you can do for them. One without the other only assures short-term success.
   —**Jeff Blackman** *Vistage Speaker*

People will crawl over broken glass for an idea but not for a number.
   —**J.P. Murray**

People's ability to change is not a function of capacity, but of choice.
   —**Morrie Shechtman** *Vistage Speaker*

Quality means doing the right thing when no one is looking.
   —**Henry Ford** *Industrialist*

Quit telling your clients what they need. Ask them what they want.
—**Sam Bowers**   *Vistage Speaker*

Quite often we change jobs, friends and spouses instead of ourselves.
—**Akbarali Jetha**   *Author*

Satisfying the customer is a race without a finish.
—**Tony Barnes**   *Vistage Speaker*

Sometimes I think I understand everything - then I regain consciousness.
—**Ray Bradbury**   *Author*

Sometimes the truth depends on a walk around the lake.
—**Wallace Stevens**   *Poet*

Spoon feeding in the long run teaches us nothing but the shape of the spoon.
—**E.M. Foster**   *Author*

Success is not something you aim for, it is something your achievements attract.
—**Unknown**

Success is often achieved by those who don't know that failure is inevitable.
—**Coco Chanel**   *Fashion Designer*

Success isn't permanent and failure isn't fatal.
—**Mike Ditka**   *Football Coach*

That is the great fallacy: the wisdom of old men. They do not grow wise, they grow careful.
—**Ernest Hemingway**   *Author*

The best ideas for improving a job come from those who do it every day.
—**Jim Bleech**   *Vistage Speaker*

In Search Of The Magic Bullet...

The big trouble with communication today, is the shortage of those willing to be communicated with.
 —**Don Fraser**

The bitter taste of low quality lingers long after the sweet taste of low price has faded.
 —***Unknown***

The CEO's job is to teach, tolerate or terminate.
 —***J. Howard Shelov*** *Vistage Speaker*

The quality of your questions determines the quality of your life.
 —***Lee Milteer*** *Author*

Customers often continue to buy for reasons different from prospects just deciding to buy.
 —***Jaynie Smith*** *Vistage Speaker*

The Colonel didn't make the gravy; Frank Smith didn't deliver the packages; your employees are your company.
 —***Frank Maguire*** *Vistage Speaker*

The customer is the most important part of the production line.
 —***W. Edwards Deming*** *Educator*

The eight last words of a dying business…"But we have always done it that way."
 —***Bud Coggins*** *Marketing Coach*

The future is no place to place your better memories.
 —***Unknown***

The future is what happens after what happens next.
 —***Ed Ryan*** *Vistage Speaker*

The greatest difficulty lies not in persuading people to accept new ideas but in persuading them to abandon old ones.
—**John Maynard Keynes** *Economist*

The greatest enemy to great is good.
—**Jim Collins** *Author*

The greatest mistake a man can make is to be afraid of making one.
—**Elbert Hubbard** *Author*

The key to success in business is to set up the organization so it's easy for the customer to do business with you.
—**Gerry Faust** *Vistage Speaker*

The level of motivation in an organization can never rise above the level of trust.
—**Clark Johnson** *Vistage Speaker*

The main thing is that you keep the main thing the main thing.
—**Albert Einstein** *Physicist*

The most essential quality for leadership is credibility - not perfection, and you build credibility by being honest, not perfect.
—**Rick Warren** *Author*

The obscure we always see sooner or later; the obvious always seems to take a little longer.
—**Edward R. Murrow** *Journalist*

The only measure of success is how much time you have to kill.
—**Nassim Taleb,** *Author*

The only easy day was yesterday.
—**Sign, US Navy Seals Training Center**

The only good thing done by a committee was the King James Version.
—**Rita Mae Brown** *Author*

The person who is waiting for something to turn up might start with their shirt sleeves.
—**Garth Henrichs**

The person who knows "how" will always have a job. The person who knows "why" will always be his boss.
—**Diane Ravitch** *Educator*

The problem in Washington today is that everybody is bargaining and nobody's negotiating.
—**Jack Kaine** *Vistage Speaker*

The purpose of credit is to get sales that otherwise would have been lost.
—**Abe Sanchez** *Vistage Speaker*

The quality of a person's life is in direct proportion to their commitment to excellence regardless of their chosen field of endeavor.
—**Vince Lombardi** *Football Coach*

The rate at which organizations learn may become the only sustainable source of competitive advantage.
—**Richard Palmer** *Vistage Speaker*

The reason to have a number is so you can decide what to change, what to leave alone.
—**Gerry Faust** *Vistage Speaker*

The reason you're as good as you are is the same reason you are only as good as you are.
—**Steven Snyder** *Vistage Speaker*

The richer your friends, the more they will cost you.
—**Elisabeth Marbury** *Author*

The right people don't think they have a job: they have responsibilities.
—*Jim Collins*   Author

If you wait, all that happens is that you get older.
—*Larry McMurtry*   Author

The road to success is lined with many tempting parking spaces.
—**Unknown**

The role of every manager should be to make each employee successful. When each employee is successful the manager and the business are successful.
—*John Perkins*   Economist

There are no absolutes. Absolutely none.
—*Richard Hanson*   SyncroFlo

The secret of managing is to keep all the guys who hate you away from those who are undecided.
—*Casey Stengel*   Baseball Manager

The significant problems we are facing cannot be solved at the same level of thinking we were at when we created them.
—*Albert Einstein*   Physicist

The trouble with research is that it tells you what people were thinking about yesterday, not tomorrow. It's like driving a car using a rearview mirror.
—*Bernard Loomis*   Toy Manufacturing Exec

The truth does not emerge from opinion.
—*David Bohm*   Physicist

The two most powerful words in any language are "What if?"
—*Kraig Kramers*   Vistage Speaker

In Search Of The Magic Bullet...

The very essence of leadership is you have to have a vision. You can't blow an uncertain trumpet.
—**Father Theodore Hesburgh**   *Notre Dame University*

There are 100 people seeking security to the one able person who is willing to risk his or her fortune.
—**J. Paul Getty**   *Industrialist*

There is only one success: to be able to spend your life in your own way.
—**Christopher Morley**   *Author*

There are no exceptions to the rule that everybody likes to be an exception to the rule.
—**Charles Osgood**   *Journalist*

There are no people on the face of the earth who embrace change as quickly as Americans.
—**Brian Beaulieu**   *Vistage Speaker*

There are some people that if they don't know you can't tell them.
—**Louis Armstrong**   *Musician*

There is a cure for every problem in the world - it's called philanthropy.
—**Steven Snyder**   *Vistage Speaker*

There is no failure in not realizing all that you might dream; the failure is not dreaming all that you might realize.
—**D. Hoc**   *Philosopher*

There is no point at which you can say "Well I am successful now. I might as well take a nap."
—**Carrie Fisher**   *Entertainer*

There is no terror in the bang, only in the anticipation of it.
—**Alfred Hitchcock**   *Media Personality*

There's no traffic jam on the extra mile.
—**Howard Hyden**   *Vistage Speaker*

There's only one person in the world who sees the business from your side of the desk.
—**Bud Carter**   *Vistage Chairman*

Things turn out best for the people who make the best of the way things turn out.
—**John Wooden**   *Basketball Coach*

Thinking outside the box is a very limiting concept.
—**Sam Bowers**   *Vistage Speaker*

We think we know what our customers want — but even they might not know until we ask.
—**Mary Lore**   *Vistage Speaker*

Those who have finished learning find themselves equipped to live in a world that no longer exists.
—**Eric Hoffer**   *Philosopher*

To achieve great things two things are needed: a plan and not quite enough time.
—**Unknown**

To catch the wave, you've got to be in the water.
—**Robert Balentine**   *Balentine*

Twenty percent of every CEO's time belongs talking to customers.
—**Jerry Goldress**   *Vistage Speaker*

We are all passengers on an aircraft we must not only fly, but redesign in flight.
—**John D. Sterman**   *Educator*

We are confronted with insurmountable opportunities.
—**Pogo**   *Cartoon Character*

In Search Of The Magic Bullet…

We love to be asked; we hate to be told.
—**Amy K Hutchens** *Vistage Speaker*

We're closest to finding ourselves just when we feel most lost.
—**Dr. Mardy Grothe** *Vistage Speaker*

Whatever it takes, that's what I do.
—**David Mellor** *Baseball Player*

When it comes to getting results, speed wins.
—**Don Schmincke** *Vistage Speaker*

When it comes to the knockdown struggle with adversity, it is a question of how many last gasps can we gasp.
—**Henry S. Haskins** *Author*

When the student is ready the teacher appears.
—**Zen Buddhist maxim**

Winners expect to win in advance. Life is a self-fulfilling prophesy.
—**Chinese Fortune Cookie**

Wisdom is the reward you get for a lifetime of listening when you'd have preferred to talk.
—**Doug Larson** *Humorist*

You can't lower your price enough to close every sale.
—**Chuck Reaves** *Vistage Speaker*

Without vision, we have no context for feedback; we're just responding to what someone else values or wants.
—**Stephen R. Covey** *Author*

It takes courage to have patience.
—**Clint Hurdle** *Baseball Manager*

Would you like me to give you a formula for success? It's quite simple really. Double your rate of failure.
—**Thomas Watson** *IBM*

Wisdom to one who is in denial is not wise.
—**Charles Lipman** *DiversiTech*

You cannot plough a field by turning it over in your mind.
—**Unknown**

You don't know what you can get away with until you try.
—**Gen. Colin Powell** *Secretary of State*

You don't need to get wet to know that it's raining.
—**Vynnie Meli** *Author*

There is no finish line
—**Arthur Blank** *Home Depot*

You have to jump off cliffs all the time and build your wings on the way down.
—**Ray Bradbury** *Author*

You might as well fall flat on your face as lean over too far backward.
—**James Thurber** *Humorist*

You really never get there because there isn't any there, there.
—**Linda Honold** *Vistage Speaker*

You should treat your employees like they can vote.
—**Daniel Amos** *Aflac*

You'll live longer if you smoke and exercise than if you don't smoke and don't exercise.
—**Larry Burback** *Vistage Speaker*

In Search Of The Magic Bullet...

You can double the profitability of an already profitable product or service with half the effort it takes to make an unprofitable product or service profitable.
　　—**Peter Drucker**　*Educator*

You can only be disappointed in people you know can do better; being disappointed in someone is really a vote of confidence in their ability to do better
　　—**Morrie Shechtman** *Vistage Speaker*

Lots of folks confuse bad management with destiny.
　　— **Kin Hubbard**　*Humorist*

How To Make Penguins Fly

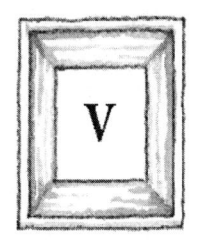

V

Brief explanations of how to
accomplish the seemingly impossible.

How To Make Penguins Fly…

You've got to play in traffic to get hit.
—**Carol Cookerly**   *Cookerly & Associates*

Your lawyer has been trained to solve problems, not create opportunities - that's not his profession.
—**Red Scott**   *Vistage Speaker*

You take people as far as they will go, not as far as you would like them to go.
—**Jeanette Rankin**   *Political Leader*

You miss 100% of the shots you don't take.
—**Wayne Gretzky**   *Hockey Player*

Important and relevant are not the same thing.
—**Brad Remillard**   *Vistage Speaker*

You manage things. You lead people.
—**Peter Drucker**   *Educator*

You have to be different in a way or a small number of ways to be important to your customers.
—**Mitch Gooze**   *Vistage Speaker*

The person who knows how will always have a job. The person who knows why will always be his boss.
—**Diane Favitch**   *Educator*

We're never not communicating.
—**Donald Phinn**   *Vistage Speaker*

You don't want to be considered just the best at what you do. You want to be known as the only one who does what you do.
—**Bill Graham**   *Concert Producer*

You can't influence anyone if they don't feel safe.
—**Dean Minuto**   *Vistage Speaker*

You can't get people to celebrate what they've accomplished until they grieve what it cost to get there.
—**Morrie Shechtman**   *Vistage Speaker*

You can accomplish anything in life provided you don't mind who gets the credit.
—**Harry Truman**   *President*

Work with the living; don't try to raise the dead.
—**David Logan**   *Vistage Speaker*

When you're in the desert, you drink the dirty water.
—**Tom Searcy**   *Vistage Speaker*

Sometimes you can measure winning by how little you lose.
—**George Stein**   *Attorney*

When you're a little bit dumb and naive things get done that no one believed could be done.
—**Unknown**

When you get to the end zone act like you've been there before.
—**Barry Sanders**   *Football Player*

When you circle the wagons, make sure all the Indians are on the outside.
—**Mike Midas**   *Vistage Chairman*

When you borrow bucks, borrow big bucks. That way if things go wrong, you've got a partner.
—**Frank Maguire**   *Vistage Speaker*

When the going gets rough the rich leave - because they can.
—**Jessie O'Neill**   *Vistage Speaker*

The world's fastest strategic planning session: Where are you? Where would you like to be? How would you like to get there?
—*Jeff Blackman*   *Vistage Speaker*

Very often there's no announcement that nothing is happening.
—*Jim Wisner*   *Financial Service Corp.*

Until your people get the "why" they don't care about the "how."
—*Gary Markle*   *Vistage Speaker*

Trust is the lubrication that makes it possible for organizations to work.
—*Warren Bennis*   *Educator*

To change an organization, change its stories.
—*Gary Hamel*   *Author*

To choose a goal without being prepared to be accountable for progress towards it is to choose nothing.
—*David Maister*   *Consultant*

Those having torches will pass them on to others.
—*Plato*   *Philosopher*

There's never been a better time to call a customer than right now.
—*Max Carey*   *Vistage Speaker*

There's a lot to be said for silence.
—*Simon Jeremiah*   *Philosopher*

There is not a person we employ who does not, like ourselves, desire recognition, praise, gentleness, forbearance and patience.
—*Henry Ward Beecher*   *Philosopher*

There is little value in the further proof of the proven.
—*Charles Lipman*   *DiversiTech*

There can be no worthwhile battle of ideas within the organization if the reward is disfavor and ill will from the boss.
—*Prof. Ray E. Brown*   *Educator*

There are two lasting bequests we can give our children. One is roots. The other is wings.
—*Hodding Carter*   *Political Leader*

There are no real secrets to success. Success in anything has one fundamental aspect: effort.
—*Sam Parker*   *Author*

There are many who want to ride the train but few willing to lay track.
—*Donald Murray*   *Children's Harbor*

You are the organization you must master.
—*Stuart Heller*   *Author*

The world makes way for the man who knows where he is going.
—*Ralph Waldo Emerson*   *Author*

Agile is the new Lean,
—*Mike Richardson* *Vistage Speaker*

The uncreative mind can spot wrong answers, but it takes a very creative mind to spot wrong questions.
—*Anthony Jay*   *Author*

The task of the leader is to get his people from where they are to where they have not been.
—*Henry Kissinger*   *Secretary of State*

The key to entrepreneurship is a willingness to live perpetually underneath a dark cloud of optimism.
—***Unknown***

The supreme accomplishment is to blur the line between work and play.
—***Arthur Toynbee***   *Philosopher*

Success is not determined by flawless execution of a plan. It is determined by how people react to failure.
—***Don Schmincke***   *Vistage Speaker*

The right to speak must be earned by having something to say.
—***Winston Churchill***   *Government Leader*

The questions you ask your sales staff determines what question they will ask your customers.
—***Chuck Reaves***   *Vistage Speaker*

The problem with popular thinking is that it doesn't require you to think at all.
—***Kevin Myers***   *Journalist*

The one who condemns the loudest is generally he who contributes the least.
—***A.G. Sertillanges***   *Author*

The new guy learns from the old guy who learned from the dead guy.
—***Scott Stratman***   *Consultant*

The mind and the heart are not motivated by small goals.
—***Steven Snyder***   *Vistage Speaker*

The man who wants to lead the orchestra must turn his back on the crowd.
—***James Crook***

Strategy is a commodity; implementation is an art.
—**Peter Drucker**   *Educator*

The highest reward for a person's toil is not what they get for it but what they become by it.
—**John Ruskin**   *Author*

The highest level of respect you can provide an individual is your undivided attention.
—**Bruce Breier**   *Vistage Speaker*

The first rule of leadership is that everything is your fault.
—**Unknown**

The first purpose of a brochure is to tell our side what we are doing.
—**David Kritzer**   *Consultant*

The difference between a deadline and a target is that one is negotiable and the other is not.
—**Bruce Breier**   *Vistage Speaker*

Our lives succeed or fail one conversation at a time.
—**Susan Scott**   *Author*

The corporate culture is the company virus - join and you can catch it.
—**Gerry Faust**   *Vistage Speaker*

The closest to perfection a person ever comes is when he fills out a job application form.
—**Stanley J. Randall**   *Author*

The biggest insult you can pay a customer is to ask them a second time for information they have already given you.
—**Jeff Bezos**   *Amazon*

Partnerships based on core competencies are the answer to today's market.
—*Alessandra Lawless*   *Creative Systems*

The best thinking has been done in solitude. The worst has been done in turmoil.
—*Thomas Edison*   *Inventor*

It is much easier to sell a customer than a prospect
—*Marty Jacknis* *Vistage Speaker*

The ability to recognize and relate, assimilate and apply principles, equals success.
—*W. Clement Stone*   *Industrialist*

That which is measured improves; that which is measured and hangs on the wall improves even more.
—*Gerry Faust*   *Vistage Speaker*

Success is simply a matter of luck. Ask any failure.
—*Earl Wilson*   *Columnist*

Really great strategies are created by individuals not teams. But implementation and execution are the work of a team.
—*Jerry Goldress*   *Vistage Speaker*

Success is often the result of taking a misstep in the right direction.
—*Al Bernstein*

Success is not for the timid. It is for those who seek guidance, make decisions and take decisive action.
—*Jose Silva*   *Author*

Somebody has to do something and it's incredibly pathetic that it has to be us.
—*Jerry Garcia*   *Musician*

See everything, overlook a great deal, and correct a little.
—**Pope John XXIII**

Results are ancient history; how are you managing the future?
—**Dan Barnett** *Vistage Speaker*

Somebody is always buying from somebody.
—**Gil Cargill** *Vistage Speaker*

Remember the airplane takes off against the wind, not with it.
—**Henry Ford** *Industrialist*

Progress is mostly the product of rogues.
—**Tom Peters** *Author*

Progress always involves risk. You can't steal second base and keep your foot on first.
—**Frederick Wilcox** *Author*

Pessimists calculate the odds. Optimists believe they can overcome them.
—**Ted Koppel** *Journalist*

People will choose to be responsible to any organization that respects them for their contribution.
—**Gerry Faust** *Vistage Speaker*

People may doubt what you say, but they will believe what you do.
—**Lewis Cass** *US Senator*

People don't want to fail on stage.
—**Bud Mingledorff** *Mingledorff's*

People don't dislike change. They dislike being changed.
—**Michael Basch** *Vistage Speaker*

People do not love change. They love inflicting change on others.
    —**Mike Murray**   *Vistage Speaker*

Ours is an age which is proud of machines that think and suspicious of men who try to.
    —***Unknown***

Only a mediocre person is always at their best.
    —**Laurence J. Peter**   *Educator*

The time to sell a mule is when the mule buyers are in town.
    —**David Borreson**   *Peachtree Builders*

One of the worst things in life is to be right too early.
    —***Unknown***

Nothing is impossible for the man who doesn't have to do it himself.
    —**A.H. Weiler**   *Film Critic*

Nothing is illegal if 100 businessmen decide to do it.
    —**Andrew Young**   *Mayor*

None of us is as smart as all of us.
    —**Ken Blanchard**   *Author*

No inanimate thing will move from one place to another without a piece of paper that goes along telling someone where to move it.
    —**Gerald E. Wilson**

Never take the advice of someone who has not had your kind of trouble.
    —**Sidney J. Harris**   *Columnist*

Never ruin an apology with an excuse.
    —**Kimberly Johnson**   *Author*

Necessity is the mother of taking chances.
—**Mark Twain** *Humorist*

Nature is so generous and kind, you just tickle her with a hoe and she laughs with a harvest.
—*Douglas Jerrold* *Journalist*

Nagging is the unending repetition of unpalatable truth.
—**Dr. Mardy Grothe** *Vistage Speaker*

Marketing is like shaving - do it every day or you're a bum.
—**Ken Cole** *Seidman & Seidman*

Management's responsibility is to identify and help employees remove roadblocks to performance.
—**Bob Thomson** *Vistage Speaker*

Management is about coping with complexity. Leadership is about coping with change.
—**Prof. John Kotter** *Harvard*

Make people believe what they think and do is important and then get out of their way while they do it.
—**Jack Welch** *General Electric*

Luck is the residue of design.
—**Branch Rickey** *Sports Executive*

Look over your shoulder now and then to be sure someone is following you.
—**Henry Gilmer**

Life is too short to spend on things you care nothing about. Make your passion your profession.
—**Les Wolff** *Wolff Sports Memorabilia*

Let people accomplish your objectives their way.
—**Clark Johnson** *Vistage Speaker*

Learn to say no. It will be of more use to you than to be able to read Latin.
—**Charles Haddon Spurgeon** *Pastor*

Leadership sets the vision for people to do the right thing. Management engineers the situation so that the easy thing is the right thing.
—**Bert Floyd** *Tune Up Clinic*

It's what you do with what you have, not what you have that counts.
—**Barry Deutsch** *Vistage Speaker*

It's not your customer's job to remember you; it's your job to make sure they don't have the opportunity to forget you.
—**Tom Feltenstein** *Vistage Speaker*

It's never too late to be what you might have been.
—**George Eliot** *Author*

It wasn't raining when Noah built the Ark.
—**Howard Ruff** *Author*

It is important to get beneath the surface before you get beneath the covers.
—**Dick Shorten** *Vistage Chairman*

It is important that people know what you stand for. It's equally as important that they know what you won't stand for.
—**Mary Waldrip**

It's your movie.
—**Paul Childs** *Vistage Speaker*

Isn't it interesting that we were brought together by business only to learn about life?
—**Walt Sutton** *Vistage Speaker*

If you're doing something you're good at that's probably bad.
—**Brad Fallon** *Vistage Speaker*

If nothing changes, nothing changes.
—**Dr. Wayne Helms** *Industrial Psychologist*

If you wish to make a man your enemy, tell him simply "you are wrong." This method works every time.
—**Henry G. Link**

If you were arrested for being a manager could they collect enough evidence to convict you?
—**Dr. Terry Paulson** *Consultant*

If you want to cook the meal, you should be allowed to buy the groceries.
—**Bill Parcels** *Football Coach*

If you want to build a ship, don't drum up the men to gather wood, divide the work and give orders. Instead, teach them to yearn for the vast and endless sea.
—**Antoine St. Exupery** *Author*

If you want to be successful do what successful companies did before they became successful - not afterwards.
—**Tom Feltenstein** *Vistage Speaker*

If you don't bring something different and better to the table the only choice you have is to be the lowest priced, and I can't see that being much fun.
—**Gordon Teel** *Georgian Bank*

If you see a snake, just kill it; don't appoint a committee on snakes.
—**H. Ross Perot** *Industrialist*

If you only give people what they already want, someone else will give them what they never dreamed possible.
— **David Ogilvie** *Advertising Executive*

If you need to be right, being an optimist is a very bad idea.
—**Steven Snyder** *Vistage Speaker*

If you listen carefully, very carefully, people will tell you where they're going, what they're willing to do. Don't assume.
—**Steve Harty** *Green Bay YMCA*

If you listen carefully you get to hear everything you didn't want to hear in the first place.
—**Sholem Aleichem** *Philosopher*

Hire for behavior; train for performance.
—**Hunter Lott** *Vistage Speaker*

If you don't know where you're going in life you're liable to wind up someplace else.
—**Yogi Berra** *Baseball Player*

I'm all in favor of planning. It's good at the end of the day to know what you didn't accomplish.
—**Bill Schwarz** *Vistage Speaker*

If you don't know what you want to do, it's harder to do it.
—**Malcolm Forbes** *Publisher*

If you don't have conflict in your company, your company is going under.
—**Morrie Shechtman** *Vistage Speaker*

If you ain't got a dream, how you gonna have a dream come true?
—**Bloody Mary** *Broadway Musical Character*

Good deals are hard to make. Bad deals are hard to break.
—**Val Dempsey** *CEI*

If we had to tolerate in others all that we permit in ourselves, life would become completely unbearable.
—**Georges Courteline** *Author*

If it had not been for the wind in my face, I wouldn't be able to fly at all.
—**Arthur Ashe** *Tennis Player*

If all possible objections must first be overcome, nothing significant will happen.
—**Clark Johnson** *Vistage Speaker*

I'd rather interview 50 people and not hire anyone than hire the wrong person.
—**Jeff Bezos** *Amazon*

I'm so caught up in my business; my personal life is going on without me.
—**Russ Walden** *Ridgewood Properties*

I had all the disadvantages required for success.
—**Larry Ellison** *Oracle*

I get my exercise acting as a pallbearer to my friends who exercise.
—**Chauncey Depew** *U. S. Senator*

I am always ready to learn, although I do not always like being taught.
—**Winston Churchill** *Government Leader*

High expectations are the key to everything.
—**Sam Walton** *Wal-Mart*

Hard work without talent is a shame, but talent without hard work is a tragedy.
—**Robert Half** *Author*

Happiness is a self inflicted condition.
—**David Hanson** *SyncroFlo*

Good ideas are not adopted automatically. They must be driven into practice with courageous patience.
—**Adm. Hyman Rickover** *Military Leader*

Going to work for a large company is like getting on a train. Are you going 60 mph or is the train going 60 mph and you're just standing still?
—**J. Paul Getty** *Industrialist*

Get the facts first. You can distort them later.
—**Mark Twain** *Humorist*

The Sales Manager's job is not to grow sales, it is to grow people.
—**Gerry Layo** *Vistage Speaker*

Going forward, people, not technology, will continue to be what counts most.
—**Richard Parsons** *AOL/Time Warner*

Given time, a seller will always tell you how to buy from him.
—**Leo Wells** *Wells Real Estate Funds*

Every single human becomes great when they set goals that inspire their heart and soul.
—**Roxanne Emmerich** *Author*

Given a reasonable opportunity, the people at the bottom will make a disproportionate contribution to the success of your company.
—**Richard Palmer** *Vistage Speaker*

Getting there is half the fun; being there is all of it.
—**Peter Sellers** *Actor*

Get rid of the bottom 5% to 10% of your customers every 90 days. Don't accept the small orders and the small margins because they can only slow you down.
—*Maurice Mascarenhas*   *Vistage Speaker*

Few things help an individual more than to place responsibility upon him and to let him know you trust him.
—**Booker Washington**   *Scientist*

Be careful how you spend your people.
—**Rick Detienne**   *Laminations*

Faced with a choice between changing one's mind and proving there is no need to do so, most everybody gets busy on the proof.
—*John Kenneth Galbraith*   *Economist*

Everyone has an invisible sign from their neck saying "make me feel important."
—**Mary Kay Ash**   *Mary Kay Cosmetics*

Every successful enterprise requires three men: a dreamer, a businessman and a son of a bitch.
—**Peter McArthur**   *Journalist*

Every new product goes through three stages: It won't work… It will cost too much… I thought it was a good idea all along.
—**Unknown**

Every man has the right to know the significance of what he is doing.
—**Russel Varian**   *The Varian Company*

Entrepreneurship is the last refuge of the trouble-making individual.
—**James K. Glassman**   *Journalist*

Education is what you get when you read the fine print; experience is what you get when you don't.
—**Pete Seeger** *Musician*

Don't spend time beating on a wall hoping to transform it into a door.
—*Coco Chanel* *Fashion Designer*

Don't worry about people stealing your ideas. If your ideas are any good you'll have to ram them down people's throats.
—*Howard Aiken* *Physicist*

Doing nothing is very hard to do; you never know when you're finished.
—*Unknown*

Do not let what you cannot do interfere with what you can do.
—*John Wooden* *Basketball Coach*

Do not fear to be eccentric in opinion for every opinion now accepted, was once eccentric.
—*Bertrand Russell* *Philosopher*

A problem well stated is a problem half solved.
—*Charles F. Kettering* *Inventor*

Dare to be awesome because the rest of the world is just average.
—*Howard Hyden* *Vistage Speaker*

Competition brings out the best in products and the worst in people.
—*David Sarnoff* *NBC*

Communication and trust rise and fall together.
—*Kraig Kramers* *Vistage Speaker*

Coming together is a beginning, staying together is progress, and working together is a success.
—**Henry Ford**   *Industrialist*

Advertising is selling Twinkies to adults.
—**Donald R. Vance**   *Author*

You can tell whether a man is clever by his answers; you can tell whether a man is wise by his questions.
—**Naguib Manfouz**   *Writer*

Change used to be a bridge to a new road - now it is the road.
—**Mark Affleck**   *California Avocados*

Being good in business is the most fascinating kind of art.
—**Andy Warhol**   *Artist*

Be generous. People will remember you for doing the things you don't have to do.
—**Renn Zaphiropoulos**   *Vistage Speaker*

Attitude is Col. Sanders getting a 30 year mortgage when he was 80 years old.
—**Frank Maguire**   *Vistage Speaker*

As long as you're going to think anyway, think big.
—**Donald Trump**   *Industrialist*

As CEOs we tend to be pathologically positive.
—**Dan Wertenberg**   *Vistage Speaker*

Argue for your limitations and sure enough, they're yours.
—**Richard Back**   *Author*

Anyone can make the simple complicated. Creativity is making the complicated simple.
—**Charles Mingus**   *Musician*

Anybody who is unwilling to spend on quality is really mapping a plan for liquidation.
—**Fred Smith** *Federal Express*

Advertising is not a panacea for all your business problems. It is a catalyst to activity.
—**Wesley Phillips** *Advertising Day*

About the time we think we can make ends meet, somebody moves the ends.
—**Herbert Hoover** *President*

A spectacular achievement is always preceded by boring preparation.
—**Unknown**

Branding is a boxer hitting one opponent 20 times and they go down; it is not one boxer hitting each of 20 opponents once.
—**Amy K Hutchens** *Vistage Speaker*

A skeptic is a person who doesn't have enough information yet to see it my way.
—**Vince Langley** *Vistage Speaker*

A reformer is a guy who rides through a sewer in a glass bottom boat.
—**James J. Walker** *Mayor*

The only thing not replicable worldwide is your people
—**Morrie Shechtman** *Vistage Speaker*

A meeting is an event in which the minutes are kept and the hours are lost.
—**Unknown**

Success is having to worry about every damn thing in the world except money.
—**Johnny Cash** *Entertainer*

Sliding Down The Razor Blade Of Life

VI

A key phrase from one of
satirist (and former Harvard Professor)
Tom Lehrer's songs evoking the pain of inevitable truths.

Your wife didn't sign up to be your congregation.
—**John Lee** *Vistage Speaker*

Your line of credit is just one phone call away from being zero.
—**Russ Walden** *Ridgewood Properties*

The only difference between a rut and a grave is the dimensions.
—**Ellen Glasgow** *Novelist*

Your business should not be an asylum for the insecure.
—**Renn Zaphiropoulos** *Vistage Speaker*

You never know when checkout time is.
—**Val Dempsey** *CEI*

You must have long range goals to keep from being frustrated by short-term failures.
—**Charles C. Noble** *Author*

You have to have purpose, you have to have vision, and most importantly, you must share it with the people in your organization.
—**Gerry Faust** *Vistage Speaker*

You don't have to be dead to write an obituary.
—**Unknown**

What is objectionable, what is dangerous, about extremists is not that they are extreme, but they are intolerant.
—**Robert F. Kennedy** *Attorney General*

You can't help getting older but you don't have to get old.
—**George Burns** *Entertainer*

We're all in this alone.
—**Lily Tomlin** *Entertainer*

You can spend a lot of money on technologies that don't fit.
—*Susan Cischke*   *Ford Motor Co*

We never seem to have enough time - yet we have all the time there is.
—*Bill Brooks*   *Vistage Speaker*

Wise men speak because they have something to say. Fools because they have to say something.
—*Plato*   *Philosopher*

Who ever heard of a fat man leading a riot?
—*Washington Irving*   *Author*

You do not lead by hitting people over the head — that's assault, not leadership.
— *Gen. Dwight D. Eisenhower*   *President*

There is no they, only us.
—*Bumper Sticker*

Where all think alike no one thinks very much.
—*Walter Lippmann*   *Journalist*

We only buy bad news.
—*Steven Snyder*   *Vistage Speaker*

When managers and leaders look at the sky at night the managers see stars, the leaders see constellations.
— *Hayward Daily Review*

When it comes to leading, there is no such thing as a trivial act.
—*Pat Murray*   *Vistage Speaker*

We must take change by the hand, or rest assuredly, change will take us by the throat.
—*Winston Churchill*   *Government Leader*

We like to judge ourselves by our good intentions, others by their performance.
—**Bob Weaver**   *Vistage Speaker*

We are the best bully the world has ever known.
—**Carlos Rizowy**   *Vistage Speaker*

We are all prisoners of our hope. No reserves, no retreat and no regrets.
—**William Borden**   *Playwright*

We are a compassionate company, but we are not Habitat for Humanity.
—**Barry Easterling**   *Healthy Life Screening*

Trashcans are full of good products and technologies that customers did not need and/or did not want to pay for.
—**Joseph Williams**   *Staircase & Millwork*

Tough times never last, but tough people do.
—**Robert H. Schuller**   *Religious Leader*

Too often we enjoy the comfort of opinion without the discomfort of thought.
—**John F. Kennedy**   *President*

Too many people stop to think and forget to start again.
—**Unknown**

Time is the enemy of all deals.
—**Susan Pravda**   *Vistage Speaker*

To get back my youth I would do anything in the world except take exercise, get up early, or be responsible.
—**Oscar Wilde**   *Author*

Those who cannot remember the past are condemned to repeat it.
—**George Santayana**   *Author*

Chairman Carter's Volume X

There's only one big event left after you retire.
—**Bobby Bowden** *Football Coach*

There's nothing worse than energizing incompetents.
—**Bill Brooks** *Vistage Speaker*

The work will wait while you show the child the rainbow, but the rainbow won't wait while you do the work.
—**Patricia Clafford** *Author*

If you're the smartest person in the room, find another room.
—**Michael Dell** *Dell Computers*

The surest way for an executive to kill himself is to refuse to learn how, and when, and to whom, to delegate work.
—**J.C. Penney** *Penney's*

There is no present or future - only the past happening over and over again - now.
—**Eugene O'Neill** *Author*

The spouting whale gets harpooned.
—**Bob Pew** *Steelcase*

There is no cure for birth or death except to enjoy the interval.
—**George Santayana** *Author*

There is no correlation linking drug use to intelligence.
—**Robert Stutman** *Vistage Speaker*

The future is here. It is not evenly distributed.
—**William Gibson** *Author*

The two most overrated things in life are the joy of natural child birth and the pleasure of owning your own business.
—*Sign in S.C. Restaurant*

The four most dangerous words in business are: All things Being Equal.
—*David Arvin*   Vistage Speaker

There is more to life than increasing its speed.
—*Mahatma Gandhi*   Political Leader

There is a lot of job security in ambiguity.
—*Leo Wells*   Wells Real Estate Funds

There are few people in life who know how to think and in our economy; the rewards are sensational for those who can make things happen.
—*Linda Wachner*   Warnaco Group

The world's best poker players don't hanker for jobs in casino management.
—*Tom Peters*   Author

The optimist proclaims that we live in the best of all possible worlds, and the pessimist fears this is true.
—*James Branch Cabell*   Author

The way we see the problem is the problem.
—*Stephen R. Covey*   Author

The truth will set you free, but first it will piss you off.
—*Gloria Steinem*   Activist

The pain of change must be less than the pain of maintaining the status quo.
—*Bob Prosen*   Vistage Speaker

The only way to get rid of a temptation is to yield to it.
—*Oscar Wilde*   Author

Start-ups are a race against insolvency.
—*Jeffrey Krida* *CruiseWest*

The only way I can tell that a new idea is really important is the feeling of terror that seizes me.
—*James Franck* *German Physicist*

Emotion in a negotiation is tantamount to giving a loaded pistol to a monkey.
— *Tom Parker* *Vistage Speaker*

The only real freedom we have is freedom of thought. We have liberties.
—*Carlos Rizowy* *Vistage Speaker*

The occupational disease of a poor executive is an inability to listen.
—*Dr. Lydia Gibers*

The measure of success is not whether you have a tough problem to deal with but whether it is the same problem you had last year.
—*John Foster Dulles* *Secretary of State*

The man who views the world at 50 the same he did at 20 has wasted 30 years of his life.
—*Mohammad Ali* *Boxer*

The man who complains about the way the ball bounces is likely the one who dropped it.
—*Lou Holtz* *Football Coach*

The longer it takes to close a deal, the less likely it is to happen; time kills deals.
—*Marisa Pensa* *Vistage Speaker*

The law does not pretend to punish everything that is dishonest. That would seriously interfere with business.
—*Clarence Darrow* *Attorney*

The future has a way of arriving unannounced.
— **George Will** *Journalist*

The fear of loss is twice the motivator as the desire for gain.
—**Dean Minuto** *Vistage Speaker*

The employer generally gets the employees he deserves.
—**Sir Walter Bilbey** *Author*

The difficulty with trust and character is that they don't show up on a balance sheet.
—**Richard Tedlow** *Author*

The difference between being a successful executive and an unsuccessful one is the difference between being right 55% of the time and being right only 49% of the time.
—*Unknown*

The 'C' students run the world.
—**Harry Truman** *President*

Tell your boss what you think of him and the truth shall set you free.
— **Hayward Daily Review**

Symptoms sometimes are the last things to show up.
—**Dr Terresa Hwang** *Feng Shui Master*

Stupid is a condition. Ignorance is a choice.
—**Wiley Miller** *Cartoonist*

'Stop doing' lists are more important than 'to do' lists.
—**Jim Collins** *Author*

Success is a lousy teacher. It seduces smart people into thinking they can't lose.
—**Bill Gates** *MicroSoft*

Speech is conveniently located midway between thought and action where it often substitutes for both.
—**John Andrew Holmes** *Author*

We punish good people by putting more and more on their plates until they break.
—**Michael Canic** *Vistage Speaker*

Sometimes the fool who rushes in gets the job done.
—**Michael LeBoeuf** *Author*

So much of what we call management consists in making it difficult for people to work.
—**Peter Drucker** *Educator*

Show me someone who has done something worthwhile and I'll show you someone who has overcome adversity.
—**Lou Holtz** *Football Coach*

Sell a man a fish, he eats for a day. Teach a man to fish; you ruin a wonderful business opportunity.
—**Karl Marx** *Political Leader*

Running a company is very easy when you don't know how, but very difficult when you do.
—**Price Pritchett** *Author*

Resentment is like taking poison and waiting for the other person to die.
—**Malachy McCourt** *Author*

Repetition does not transform a lie into the truth.
—**Franklin D. Roosevelt** *President*

Real power in an organization is held by those who have the capacity to grant and withhold cooperation.
—**Peter Schutz** *Vistage Speaker*

Sliding Down The Razor Blade Of Life…

Publicity is like poison. It doesn't hurt unless you swallow it.
—**Joe Paterno** *Football Coach*

Philosophy drives attitude, which drives action, which drives results, which drive lifestyle. If you have a problem with your lifestyle, check your philosophy.
—**Jim Rohn** *Author*

People only tell the truth one of two ways: anonymously or posthumously.
—**Dr. Mardy Grothe** *Vistage Speaker*

People issues are the crabgrass in the lawn of business.
—**Russ Walden** *Ridgewood Properties*

People get hired for what they know and fired for who they are.
—**Ed Ryan** *Vistage Speaker*

People are known by the company they keep; companies are known by the people they keep.
—**Bill Gates** *Microsoft*

Partnerships are not made in the womb.
—**Bud Mingledorff** *Mingledorff's*

Social, technological, economic environmental an political issues can kill your company as easily as running out of cash.
—**Michael Canic** *Vistage Speaker*

Pain is never permanent.
—**Saint Teresa of Avila**

Pain is inevitable; suffering is optional.
—**Dr. Hermann Witte** *Vistage Speaker*

One of the greatest diseases is to be nobody to anybody.
—**Mother Teresa** *Humanitarian*

One lifetime isn't enough. Just when you start to learn, it's time to go.
—**Luis Marden** *National Geographic*

One fifth of the people are against everything all the time.
—**Robert F. Kennedy** *Attorney General*

Old age occurs when your attachment to the past exceeds your excitement for the future.
—**Unknown**

Obstacles are those frightful things you see when you take your eyes off the goal.
—**Hannah Moore** *Philanthropist*

Obsessive cost control is the embalming fluid of business today.
—**Tom Feltenstein** *Vistage Speaker*

No organization can make good decisions without conflict.
—**Ian MacDougall** *Vistage Speaker*

Nobody succeeds beyond his or her wildest expectations unless he or she begins with some wild expectations.
—**Ralph Charell** *Author*

Man is still the most inexpensive, nonlinear, all-purpose computing system that is capable of being mass produced by unskilled labor.
—**Unknown**

Nothing recedes like success.
—**Walter Winchell** *Columnist*

Sliding Down The Razor Blade Of Life…

No one knows enough to be a pessimist.
—**Tom Feltenstein** *Vistage Speaker*

No one can guess the future loss of business from a dissatisfied customer.
—**W. Edwards Deming** *Educator*

If it works, it's obsolete.
—**Marshall McLuhan** *Author*

Never let anyone tell you 'no' who doesn't have the power to say 'yes.'
—**Eleanor Roosevelt** *U.N. Delegate*

Never ascribe to malice that which can adequately be explained by incompetence.
—**Napoleon Bonaparte** *Government Leader*

Near-death experiences are very healthy for companies.
—**David Cole** *Center for Automotive Research*

My interest is in the future because I am going to spend the rest of my life there.
—**Charles F. Kettering** *Inventor*

My daddy told me that when someone says 'it isn't about the money, it's the principle of the thing,' it is always about the money.
—**Leonard Rosen** *Financial News Network*

Most see what is before them, the strategic leaders' sense what is around the corner.
—**Kirby Martzall** *Vistage Chairman*

Most companies do an exceptional job of attracting the top people in the bottom third of the talent pool.
—**Brad Remillard** *Vistage Speaker*

Let us be thankful for the fools. But for them the rest of us could not succeed.
—**Mark Twain** *Humorist*

Most people who own their own businesses are not entrepreneurs - they are technicians who suffered a seizure.
—**Michael Gerber** *Author*

If you're done getting better, retire.
—**Ken Favizza** *Sports Psychologist*

Most CEOs require less of their top lieutenants than they do of themselves.
—**Del Poling** *Vistage Speaker*

Life is like a roll of toilet paper, the closer it gets to the end, the faster it goes.
—**Andy Rooney** *Journalist*

Life is like a 10-speed bicycle. Most of us have gears we never use.
—**Charles Schulz** *Cartoonist*

Life is a grindstone. Whether it grinds you down or polishes you up depends on what you are made of.
—**Unknown**

Life is a great big canvas; throw all the paint on it you can.
—**Danny Kaye** *Entertainer*

Life can only be understood backward but it must be lived forward.
—**Soren Kierkegaard** *Philosopher*

Light travels faster than sound. That's why some people appear bright until you hear them speak.
—**Unknown**

Leading edge technology can easily become bleeding edge technology.
  —**Donald Luger** Lockwood Greene

Leadership, among other things, is the ability to inflict short-term pain for long-term gain.
  —**George Will** *Journalist*

Leadership is about change.
  —**Don Schmincke** *Vistage Speaker*

LBOs are financed by the past. IPOs are financed by the future.
  —**Gregory Edwards**

Just think how happy you would be if you lost everything you have right now, and then got it back again.
  —**Frances Rodman** *Author*

Just be yourself. Everyone else is taken.
  —**Lowell Nerenberg** *Vistage Chairman*

Your sales people leave money on the table because they want to be liked.
  —**Bob Gibson** *Vistage Speaker*

It's just your money not your life. Everybody who really loved you a week ago still loves you tonight.
  —**Louis Rukeyser** *Media Personality*

It's better to be rejected by a process rather than a person.
  —**Charles Lipman** *DiversiTech*

It is far better to be shot from a cannon than squeezed from a tube.
  —**Harry Truman** *President*

In business, "wait" is a four-letter word.
—*Comcast advertising slogan*

In this "house" it is the right of each one to have identity, equity and opportunity. A business is rightly judged by its product and service - but must also face scrutiny and judgment as to its humanity.
—*D.J. DePree* Herman Miller

If your horse dies, get off.
—*Sign in Kentucky field*

In the real world all flat tires must be fixed while moving.
—*Dr. Terry Paulson* Consultant

If you don't think too good, don't think too much.
—*Ted Williams* Baseball Player

In life, you think you should have blueprints and specifications, but all you have in life is a bunch of change orders and duct tape.
—*Terry England* England Bros. Construction

In economic growth, as in auto racing, it's not the speed that kills; it's the sudden stop.
—*Robert Rodriquez* FPA Capital

If you're not living on the edge you're taking up too much space.
—*Tom Feltenstein* Vistage Speaker

The ultimate form of abandonment is accepting people as they are.
—*Morrie Shechtman* Vistage Speaker

If you're in a leadership position and your subordinate staff isn't cutting it, replace your subordinates or your replacement will.
—*Jeff Vogelsang* Vistage Speaker

Sliding Down The Razor Blade Of Life…

If you're not a cynic by the time you've reached 30 you just haven't been paying attention.
  —Bob Friedman

I'm not always right but I'm never in doubt.
  —Red Scott *Vistage Speaker*

If you serve the classes you dine with the masses. But if you service the masses you'll dine with the classes.
  —Unknown

If you live in the ocean and don't have gills, I suspect you may have reason for concern.
  —Pete Coriell *Georgia Pacific*

If you have everything under control you're not going fast enough.
  —Mario Andretti *Race Car Driver*

If you have a job without aggravation you don't have a job.
  —Malcolm Forbes *Publisher*

If you can't sell a top quality product at the world's lowest price, you're going to be out of the game.
  —Jack Welch *General Electric*

If you don't stand for something, chances are good you will fall for anything.
  —Lois Fincher

If you don't like change you are going to like irrelevance a lot less.
  —Tom Feltenstein *Vistage Speaker*

If you don't cope well with stress, you don't stay well.
  —Dr. Jerry Kornfield *Vistage Speaker*

If you can't control somebody, you better be able to trust them.
—*Donald Phinn* *Vistage Speaker*

Throwing somebody into the deep to test their skills isn't delegation… it's hazing.
—*Dr. James Crubman* *Consultant*

If you believe the only thing you can control are the activities, you are saying you don't matter.
—*Gerry Faust* *Vistage Speaker*

If you are what you do, what are you when you don't?
—*Richard Nixon* *Vistage Speaker*

If you are not careful your success in the past will block your chances to succeed in the future.
—*Joel A. Barker* *Consultant*

If we don't change our direction we're likely to end up where we're headed.
—*Chinese Proverb*

If there's no such thing as risk of loss, there is no potential for gain.
—*Leo Wells* *Wells Real Estate Funds*

If sales people are left to their own devices they will invariably go after the low hanging fruit.
—*Jim Cecil* *Vistage Speaker*

If bullshit were music some people would be marching bands.
—*Charlie King* *King Industrial Realty*

I worry most what my people don't know that they don't know.
—*Stanley Davis* *Consultant*

Sliding Down The Razor Blade Of Life…

It's easy to make a buck. It's a lot tougher to make a difference.
    —**Tom Brokaw** *Journalist*

I want a nice guy for a neighbor, not a direct report.
    —**Jeff Vogelsang**   *Vistage Speaker*

I really enjoy good 'crash and burn' stories; I just don't like to be in them.
    —**Charles Smithgall**   *Aaron's*

I love America more than any other country in this world, and exactly for this reason, I insist on the right to criticize her perpetually.
    —**James Baldwin**   *Author*

I have never seen a monument erected to a pessimist.
    —**Paul Harvey** *Commentator*

I have an open door policy, but please don't come in.
    —**Bortie Twiford** *B&R Associates*

I don't want any yes men around me. I want everybody to tell me the truth even if it costs them their job.
    —**Samuel Goldwyn** *Businessman*

I don't care to be involved in the crash landing unless I can be in on the takeoff.
    —**Harold Stassen** *Governor*

I am convinced that if the rate of change inside an organization is less than the rate of change outside, the end is in sight.
    —**Jack Welch** *General Electric*

Hurt people, hurt people.
    —**Unknown**

How come every time I get stabbed in the back, my fingerprints are on the knife?
  —*Dr. Jerry Harvey* *Vistage Speaker*

Hire slowly; terminate quickly.
  —*Ed Ryan* *Vistage Speaker*

Events over which you have no control are having a greater and greater influence on your business.
  —*Herb Meyer* *Vistage Speaker*

Happiness comes from moving towards getting what you want; not from getting it.
  —*Steven Snyder* *Vistage Speaker*

Good times are very tolerant of bad management.
  —*Sheldon Stahl* *Vistage Speaker*

Give up the hope of a better past.
  —*Irvin Yalom* *Author*

Freedom is the freedom to discipline yourself so others don't have to.
  —*John Wooden* *Basketball Coach*

Forget about price, forget about service. How you handle your customers' problems determines your customers' loyalty.
  —*Michael Basch* *Vistage Speaker*

Ford used to have a better idea, now they don't have a clue.
  —*Steve Kravitz* *Comedian*

Following the path of least resistance is what makes rivers and men crooked.
  —*Unknown*

Finish your homework. People in China and India are starving for your job.
—**Thomas Freidman** *Author*

Feeling is what you get for thinking the way you do.
—**Marilyn vos Savant** *Columnist*

Failure can be bought on easy terms; success must be paid for in advance.
—**Cullen Hightower** *Author*

Facts do not cease to exist because they are ignored.
—**Aldous Huxley** *Author*

Every day, some ordinary person does something extra ordinary. Today, it's your turn.
—**Lou Holtz** *Football Coach*

Experience is not what happens to a man. It is what a man does with what happens to him.
—**Aldous Huxley** *Author*

Experience is a hard teacher because she gives the test first the lesson afterwards.
—**Vernon Law** *Baseball Player*

Everything I've learned about life I can sum up in three words: it goes on.
—**Robert Frost** *Poet*

Even if I knew that tomorrow the world would go to pieces, I would still plant my apple tree.
—**Martin Luther** *Philosopher*

By the time we make it, we've had it.
—**Malcolm Forbes** *Publisher*

Eighty percent of the illnesses we get are self-inflicted.
—**Dr. Jerry Kornfield** *Vistage Speaker*

As an organization grows and succeeds, it sows the seeds of its own demise by getting boring.
—**Seth Godin** *Author*

Don't undress until you're ready for bed.
—**Larry Knecht** *Attorney*

Don't tell them more than you know.
—**Al Neuharth** *USA Today*

Don't book a $1000 meeting to solve a $100 problem.
— **Maurice Mascarenhas** *Vistage Speaker*

Bad news never gets better with time.
—**Adm. Hyman Rickover** *Military Leader*

Documentation is like sex; when it's good, it's very good and when it's bad, it's better than nothing.
—**Dick Brandon** *Author*

At the feast of ego, everyone leaves hungry.
—**Sign in Tucson coffee house.**

Be nice to your kids. They'll choose your nursing home.
—**Unknown**

Communication is to leadership, as the swing is to golf; everyone can do it, but few do it well.
—**Don A. Sanders** *Author*

Everyone is gifted. Some just never open their packages.
—**Steven Snyder** *Vistage Speaker*

Change is an emotional event. If it don't make you want to go to the sink and puke, it probably ain't worth doing.
—**Ralph Stayer** *Johnsonville Meats*

Business is like riding a bicycle. Either you keep moving or you fall off.
—**John David Wright**

Sliding Down The Razor Blade Of Life...

Big will not beat small anymore; it will be the fast beating the slow.
  —**Rupert Murdoch** *Industrialist*

Be thankful for the troubles of your job because if it weren't for the things that go wrong, someone could handle your job for half of what you're getting paid to do it.
  —**Unknown**

Avoid litigation. When was the last time you saw a jury composed of company presidents?
  —**Michael Lotito** *Vistage Speaker*

A really effective leader will run out of answers long before he runs out of questions.
  —**Bob Thomas** *Vistage Speaker*

Attitudes are caught, not taught.
  —**Maurice Mascarenhas** *Vistage Speaker*

At some time in the life cycle of virtually every organization its ability to succeed, in spite of itself, runs out.
  —**Richard H. Brien** *Author*

Anyone who says businessmen deal only in facts, not fiction, has never read any five-year growth projections.
  —**Malcolm Forbes** *Publisher*

An appeaser is one who feeds a crocodile - hoping it will eat him last.
  —**Winston Churchill** *Government Leader*

All the major causes of death are self-inflicted.
  —**Joe Dillon** *Vistage Speaker*

A true leader always keeps an element of surprise up his sleeve which others cannot grasp but which keeps his public excited and breathless.
—*Charles De Gaulle*   Political Leader

A partner is someone who goes to the bank with you and watches you sign a personal guarantee for more money than you have.
—*Gerry Faust*   Vistage Speaker

A government big enough to give you everything you want is a government big enough to take away everything you have.
—*Gerald Ford*   President

A good recession only comes along once in a lifetime...we need to take advantage of it.
—*Barry Schimel*   Vistage Speaker

A salary is an anachronism in our time. It should have died with the factory system. It is idiotic to pay someone guaranteed money when there is no guarantee for the owner.
—*Morrie Shechtman*   Vistage Speaker

A company can make a social contribution only if it is highly profitable.
—*Peter Drucker*   Educator

Slaying Life's Goliaths

VII

A few pebbles for your
business' slingshot.

Managers are people who do things right and leaders are people who do the right thing.
—**Warren Bennis & Burt Nanus** *Authors*

You have to have a dream so you can get up in the morning.
—**Billy Wilder** *Film Maker*

The worst thing about fear is the fear it's going to get worse.
—**Steven Snyder** *Vistage Speaker*

You have to be smarter than the door to open it.
—**Morgan Rogers**

You can't kill a man born to hang.
—**Restaurant chain slogan**

You can always see what goes wrong but you can't see the cause. Causes are invisible.
—**Bill Schwarz** *Vistage Speaker*

To create you must first destroy.
—**Picasso** *Artist*

You are either the leader or you are led.
—**Carlos Rizowy** *Vistage Speaker*

When your work speaks for itself, don't interrupt.
—**Harry Kaiser** *Industrialist*

When you win, nothing hurts.
—**Joe Namath** *Football Player*

When land was the scarce resource, nations battled over it…the same is happening now for talented people.
—**Stan Davis** *Consultant*

What would you attempt to do if you knew you could not fail?
—*Unknown*

We're all ignorant just on different subjects.
—*Will Rogers* Humorist

Unless you walk out into the unknown the odds of making a profound difference in your life are pretty low.
—*Tom Peters* Author

We ask people to change without showing them what they can become.
—*Sheila Sheinberg* Vistage Speaker

Waste money in a business and you may ultimately be able to recoup it; waste time in a business and it is gone forever. Make your plans around time, not money.
—*Peter Schutz* Vistage Speaker

A wise man gets more from his enemies than a fool from his friends.
—*Baltasar Gracian* philosopher

Values are like fingerprints - nobody's are the same, but you leave 'em all over everything you do.
—*Elvis Presley* Entertainer

There's always an "until."
—*Leo Wells* Wells Real Estate Funds

There's no such thing as "wrongful discharge." They're all wrongful hires.
—*Michael Lotito* Vistage Speaker

There is nothing more vulnerable than entrenched success.
—*George Romney* Governor

Slaying Life's Goliaths…

There is no limit to what a man can do or where he can go if he doesn't mind who gets the credit.
  —**Robert Woodruff** *Coca Cola*

There is no great fun, satisfaction, or joy derived from doing something that's easy.
  —***John Wooden*** *Basketball Coach*

The Gross National product would be 10 times what it is today were everything people put on their resumes true.
  —***Marty Jacknis*** *Vistage*

There are only three colors, ten digits, and seven notes; it's what we do with them that's important.
  —***Jim Rohn*** *Author*

There are few sorrows, however poignant, in which a good income is of no avail.
  —***Logan Piersall Smith*** *Essayist*

The value of your product is equal to the cost of your customer's problem.
  —***Chuck Reaves*** *Vistage Speaker*

The single greatest factor effecting our happiness is the level at which you live in congruence with your personal values.
  —***Bob Weaver*** *Vistage Speaker*

The next time you quit would you please resign on the same day.
  —***Sign in Nordstrom employee lounge***

The secret of a successful organization is to get ordinary people to do extraordinary things.
  —***Peter Schutz*** *Vistage Speaker*

The reason why everybody likes planning is because nobody has to do anything.
—**Edmund G. Brown** *Governor*

The quality of the leader is reflected in the standards they set for themselves.
—**Ray Kroc** *McDonalds*

The most dangerous people in your organization are the very successful people who don't align with your beliefs.
—**Don Schmincke** *Vistage Speaker*

The quality of any product or service is what the customer says it is.
—**Techsonic**

We can't all be heroes because someone has to sit on the curb and clap as they go by.
— **Will Rogers** *Humorist*

The goal of parenting is that one day, as you stand in the doorway; your kids give you the finger and ride off into the sunset.
—**Morrie Shechtman** *Vistage Speaker*

I hire people smarter than me and then I get out of the way.
—**Lee Iacocca** *Industrialist*

The sale begins when the customer says "yes".
—**Harvey Mackay** *Author*

The people who do business with you pay for those who don't.
—**William McBurney** *The McBurney Company*

The human mind is the worst possible place to store business information.
—**Konichi Ohmae** *Consultant*

The only sense that is common in the long run is the sense of change - and we all instinctively avoid it.
—**E.B. White** *Author*

The only means of strengthening of one's intellect is to make up one's mind about nothing - to let the mind be a thoroughfare for all thoughts.
—***John Keats*** *Author*

Success involves turning habits into culture.
—***Emile Blau*** *Restaurateur*

The old adage "people are your most important asset" turns out to be wrong. People are not your most important asset. The RIGHT people are.
—***Jim Collins*** *Author*

The nicest thing about not planning is that failure comes as a complete surprise and is not preceded by a period of worry and depression.
—***Richard Palmer*** *Vistage Speaker*

The money you have will give you freedom. The money you pursue will enslave you.
—***Rousseau*** *Philosopher*

The key to satisfaction and motivation is basic human decency. Humans are at least as bright and sensitive as houseplants. Treat them well and they'll flourish.
—***Joe Anderson*** *Vistage Chairman*

The issues of the CEO inevitably re-emerge as issues within the organization.
—***James Newton*** *Vistage Speaker*

The happiest of lives are only splendid wrecks of what used to be a future.
—***Gore Vidal*** *Author*

The downfall of the magician is belief in his own magic.
—**Russ Walden** *Ridgewood Properties*

The deepest principle of human nature is the craving to be appreciated.
—**William James** *Author*

The company with the best information wins all the time.
—**Pat Price**

The collegiality in your business can be a real barrier to the openness required to identify and deal with your tough issues.
—**Craig Weber** *Vistage Speaker*

The biggest mistake a man in management can make is to back down on a matter of principle.
—**Clarence Francis** *General Foods*

The bigger a man's head gets, the easier it is to fill his shoes.
—**Henry Courtney**

Sometimes you have to be able to step on their toes without messing up their shine.
—**Unknown**

People change and forget to tell each other.
—**Lillian Hellman** *Author*

Sometimes it's hard getting out of bed when you're wearing silk pajamas.
—**Willie Shoemaker** *Jockey*

Slumps are like a soft bed. They're easy to get into and hard to get out of.
—**Johnny Bench** *Baseball Player*

Slaying Life's Goliaths...

Regret and fear are twin thieves who rob us of today.
—**Robert J. Hastings** *Author*

Production of useful work is limited by the laws of thermodynamics, but the production of useless work seems to be unlimited.
—**Donald Simanek** *Physicist*

Practice without improvement is meaningless.
—**Chuck Knox** *Football Coach*

Power is always dangerous. Power attracts the worst and corrupts the best.
—**Edward Abbey** *Author*

Nobody roots for Goliath.
—**Wilt Chamberlain** *Basketball Player*

People work harder, longer and better if they believe their work is meaningful and positive.
—**Rick Richard** *Columbia Gas System*

People will forget what you say; people will even forget what you did, but people will never forget how you made them feel.
—**Joe Pine** *Author*

Nothing fails like success.
—**Jim Sandstrom** *Vistage Speaker*

People want economy and they will pay any price to get it.
—**Lee Iacocca** *Industrialist*

People prefer a problem they don't like to an answer they don't like.
—**Lee Thayer** *Vistage Speaker*

People like to use the word 'guru' only because they don't want to say 'charlatan.'
—*Peter Drucker*   Educator

People do not fear the unknown. They fear the unstated known.
—**Morrie Shechtman**   Vistage Speaker

People can live longer without food than without information.
—**Arthur C. Clarke**   Author

People are like string. You can pull them along but you can't push them.
—**Unknown**

Once power was considered a masculine attribute. In fact, power has no sex.
—**Katherine Graham**   Publisher

Much of what we call management today consists of making it difficult for people to work.
—**Peter Drucker**   Educator

Most people tip-toe through life hoping they make it safely to death.
—**Earl Nightingale**   Broadcast Philosopher

Once the game is over, the king and the pawn go back in the same box.
—**Unknown**

Most businesses expand at the peak of the business cycle when prices are at their highest.
—**Brian Beaulieu**   Vistage Speaker

Money is like manure; it should be spread around.
—**Brooke Astor**   Philanthropist

It's a funny thing about life: If you refuse to accept anything but the best you very often get it.
—**W. Somerset Maugham**   *Author*

Creating a business that can be profitable no matter the environmental conditions requires as much attention to culture as it does cost structure.
—*Andy Fleming*   *Vistage Speaker*

Money is always there, but the pockets change.
—*Gertrude Stein*   *Author*

Managers must have the discipline not to keep pulling up the flowers to see if the roots are healthy.
—*Robert Townsend*   *Author*

Manage your business to increase value, not sales.
—*Peter Collins*   *Vistage Speaker*

Man will occasionally stumble over the truth but most of the time he will pick himself up and continue on.
—*Winston Churchill*   *Government Leader*

Make sure you're finished speaking before your audience has finished listening.
—*Dorothy Sarnoff*   *Consultant*

Loved my horse. Shot him of course!
—*Alan Goodhue*   *Poet*

Life isn't about waiting for the storm to pass. It's about learning to dance in the rain.
—*Unknown*

Life begins at the edge of your comfort zone.
—*Jim Madrid*   *Entelechy*

Leave some money on the table.
—*Craig Newmark*   *Craigslist*

I've found that luck is quite predictable. If you want more luck take more chances. Be more active. Show up more often.
—*Brian Tracy*   *Author*

I've developed a new philosophy...I only dread one day at a time.
—*Charlie Brown*   *Cartoon Character*

It is always your next move.
—*Napoleon Hill*   *Author*

It's a lot harder to steal someone away from a career than it is to steal them from a job.
—*Gary Markle*   *Vistage Speaker*

It is only when the tide goes out that you see who was swimming without shorts.
—*Warren Buffet*   *Industrialist*

It is easy to get to the top after you get through the crowd at the bottom.
—*Zig Ziglar*   *Trainer*

Intelligent people, when assembled into an organization, will tend toward collective stupidity.
—*Karl Albrecht*   *Author*

Inside an organization there are only cost centers. The only profit center is a customer whose check has not bounced.
—*Peter Drucker*   *Educator*

In this day and age, if you are not confused, you are not thinking clearly.
—*Burt Nanus*   *Author*

If your salesmen aren't getting 'no' enough they're either on vacation or order takers.
—*Marisa Pensa*   *Vistage Speaker*

In business, the guy in the middle dies.
 —**Gideon Malherbe** *Vistage Speaker*

If each of us hires people who are smaller that we are, we shall become a company of dwarfs, but if each of us hires people who are bigger than we are, we shall become a company of giants.
 —**David Ogilvie** *Ogilvie Agency*

If you're too busy to learn you won't be busy for very long.
 —**Unknown**

If you want to run with the big dogs, you've got to stop pissing like a puppy.
 —**Leon White** *Vistage Member*

Affluence means influence.
 —**Jack London** *Author*

If you do not develop a strategy on your own, you become part of someone else's strategy.
 —**Alvin Toffler** *Futurist*

If you can't see the path in front of you laid out step by step, then it's not your path.
 —**Joseph Campbell** *Author*

Feeling enthusiastic usually leads to inventory.
 —**Bob Taggart** *Chaparral Communications*

If you can persuade your customer to tattoo your name on their chest, they probably will not ever switch brands.
 — **Unknown**

If we did all the things we are capable of doing we would literally astonish ourselves.
 —**Thomas Edison** *Inventor*

I know God won't give me anything I can't handle. I just wish he didn't trust me so much.
—**Mother Teresa** *humanitarian*

If we can, why wouldn't we?
—***Unknown***

I can't tell you how to make a deal, but I can tell you that if you don't work on it, you won't make it.
—**Charlie King** *King Industrial Realty*

I can't remember a day when I've gotten done.
—**Gerry Faust** *Vistage Speaker*

Give me six hours to chop down a tree and I will spend the first four sharpening the axe.
—**Abraham Lincoln** *President*

Get good before you get big. It's awfully hard to get good after you get big.
—***Unknown***

Experience tells you what to do; confidence allows you to do it.
—**Stan Smith** *Tennis Player*

Executive ability is the talent for deciding something quickly and getting somebody else to do it.
—**Red Scott** *Vistage Speaker*

Everyone who got where he is, had to begin where he was.
—**Robert Louis Stevenson** *Author*

Egotism is the only disease known to mankind that affects everyone except the carrier.
—**Red Scott** *Vistage Speaker*

Don't cry because it is over...smile because it happened.
—**Dr. Suess**   *Fictional Character*

Don't skate to where the puck is — skate to where the puck is going to be.
—**Wayne Gretzky**   *Hockey Player*

Don't forget until too late that the business of life is not business, but living.
—**B.C. Forbes**   *Journalist*

Do not allow what is very good to keep you from what is best.
—**Tom Morris**   *Educator*

Customers may not know or care how quickly you did a job but they will always care how well you did it.
—**William Spoor**   *Pillsbury Company*

Bad things happen...Life depends on how you deal with them.
—**Larry Siedlick**   *Sunrise Medical Labs*

Calling yourself a professional no more makes you a professional than sitting in your garage makes you a car.
—**Bob Weber**   *Vistage Speaker*

Business doesn't function the way you read about it in the books.
—**Don Schmincke**   *Vistage Speaker*

Be quick, but don't hurry.
—**John Wooden**   *Basketball Coach*

Be kind. Everyone you meet is fighting a hard battle.
—**Lee Dushoff**   *Consultant*

Be careful that your competitors don't make gourmet hamburger out of your company's sacred cows.
—**Unknown**

A leader is one who knows the way, goes the way, and shows the way.
—**John Maxwell** *Author*

At any moment during a 24 hour day, only one third of the people in the world are asleep. The other two-thirds are awake and creating problems.
—**Adm. Hyman Rickover** *Military Leader*

As a novelist, I tell stories and people give me money. Then financial planners tell me stories, and I give them money.
—**Martin Cruze Smith** *Author*

An organization that runs like clockwork is great but only if its goal is to run around in the same circles forever.
—**Unknown**

America is the land of opportunity if you're a businessman in Japan.
—**Laurence J. Peter** *Educator*

All business in a democratic country begins with public permission and exists by public approval.
—**Arthur W. Page** *AT & T*

Changing your life is an inside job.
—**Maureen Mulvaney** **Vistage Speaker**

A ship in port is safe, but that's not what ships are built for.
—**Grace Hopper** *Inventor*

A real leader faces the music, even when he doesn't like the tune.
—**Unknown**

Let's Get Serious About Humor

VIII

Humor, appropriately applied in the workplace, can mean bigger deposits at the bank. Work should be fun.

Let's Get Serious About Humor...

You only lie to two people in your life: your girlfriend and the police. Everybody else you tell the truth to.
—**Jack Nicholson**   *Actor*

You may not realize it when it happens but a kick in the teeth may be the best thing in the world for you.
—**Walt Disney**   *Industrialist*

You don't have to be nice to people on the way up if you're not coming back down.
—**Col. Tom Parker**   *Personal Manager*

A common mistake people make when trying to design something completely foolproof is to underestimate the ingenuity of completer fools.
—**Douglas Adams**   *Humorist*

You can marry more money in five minutes than you can earn in a lifetime of hard work.
—**Arthur P. Laws**

You can live to be 100 if you want to give up all the things that make you want to live to be 100.
—**Woody Allen**   *Entertainer*

You can go a long way with a smile. You can go a lot further with a smile and a gun.
—**Al Capone**   *Gangster*

You can fool some of the people all of the time and that's enough to make a profit.
—**Unknown**

You can always spot a well-informed man - his views are the same as yours.
—**Ilka Chase**   *Actress*

Work eight hours and sleep eight hours and make sure that they are not the same hours.
—**T. Boone Pickens**   *Industrialist*

Wit has truth in it; wise-cracking is simply calisthenics with words.
—*Dorothy Parker*   Humorist

Why not go out on a limb? That's where the fruit is.
—*Will Rogers*   Humorist

Why is it there's never enough time to do the job right, but there's always enough time to do it over.
—*Unknown*

Wherever I go, I have to take myself - and that spoils everything.
—*Dr. Murray Banks*   Psychologist

When you need a friend it's too late to make one.
—*Mark Twain*   Humorist

When you are arguing with a fool make sure he is not doing the same thing.
—*Unknown*

When they raid the whorehouse they take the piano player too.
—*Unknown*

When the effective leader is finished with his work, the people say it happened naturally.
—*Lao Tse*   Philosopher

Whenever you got business trouble the best thing to do is to get a lawyer. Then you got more trouble, but at least you got a lawyer.
—*Chico Marx*   Comedian

Whatever picture you paint in your mind the body goes to work to complete.
—*Unknown*

Let's Get Serious About Humor...

We can lick gravity but sometimes the paperwork is overwhelming.
—**Wernher Von Braun**   *Scientist*

The older I get the better I was.
—**Sandy Koufax**   *Baseball Player*

Voters think Washington is a whorehouse and every four years they get a chance to elect a new piano player.
—**Peggy Noonan**   *Journalist*

Vision is very important because you have to have a path where the company is going to go. But visions that you don't execute are called hallucinations.
—**John Roth**   *Nortel Networks*

Time is that thing in nature which prevents everything from happening all at once. Lately it doesn't seem to be working.
—**Unknown**

Thunder is good, thunder is impressive, but it's lightning that does the work.
—**Mark Twain**   *Humorist*

Those things people say you can't get along without, we used to live without.
—**Unknown**

Things will get better - despite our efforts to improve them.
—**Will Rogers**   *Humorist*

Things are more like they are now, than they have ever been.
—**Gerald Ford**   *President*

There are very few people I trust in this world and I'm not one of them.
—**Richard Grimes**   *Grimes Finishings Ltd*

There are three kinds of men. The one that learns by reading. The few who learn by observation. And the rest of them have to pee on the electric fence for themselves.
—**Will Rogers** *Humorist*

The income tax has made liars out of more Americans than golf.
—**Will Rogers** *Humorist*

The way I see it, if you want a rainbow, you gotta put up with the rain.
—**Dolly Parton** *Entertainer*

The trouble with unemployment is that the minute you wake up in the morning you are on the job.
—**Slappy White** *Entertainer*

The road to success is always under construction.
—**Lily Tomlin** *Entertainer*

The only reason a great many American families don't own an elephant is that they have never been offered an elephant for a dollar down and easy weekly payments.
—**Unknown**

The only one who welcomes change is a wet baby.
—**Unknown**

The only nice thing about being imperfect is the joy it brings to others.
—**Doug Larson** *Humorist*

The most terrifying words in the English language are: I'm from the government and I'm here to help.
—**Ronald Reagan** *President*

The biggest impact of technology has been to allow us to do more unproductive things at a far more impressive rate...
—**Scott Adams** *Cartoonist*

Let's Get Serious About Humor...

The most efficient labor saving device is still money.
 —**Unknown**

The handwriting on the wall may be a forgery.
 —**Ralph Hodgson** *Poet*

The meek shall inherit the earth but not its mineral rights.
 —**J. Paul Getty** *Industrialist*

The higher you climb the flagpole, the more people see your rear end.
 —**Don Meredith** *Football Player*

The habitually punctual make all their mistakes right on time.
 —**Laurence J. Peter** *Educator*

The government is like a baby's alimentary canal with a happy appetite at one end and no responsibility at the other.
 —**Ronald Reagan** *President*

A boat is an anchor.
 —**Frank Forencich** *Scholar*

The economy of Houston is so bad right now that two prostitutes the police arrested turned out to be virgins.
 —**Bill Abeel** *Journalist*

The differences between this place and a hedgehog is that the hedgehog has all the pricks on the outside.
 —**Graffito**

The closest anyone ever comes to perfection is on a job application.
 —**Unknown**

The brain is a wonderful organ. It starts the moment you get up and doesn't stop until you get into the office.
—**Robert Frost** *Poet*

Talk low, talk slow and don't say very much.
—*John Wayne* *Actor*

Talk is cheap because supply exceeds demand.
—***Unknown***

Start each day with a smile and get it over with.
—**W.C. Fields** *Entertainer*

Sometimes I get the feeling the whole world is against me, but deep down I know that's not true. Some of the smaller countries are neutral.
—**Bob Orben** *Humorist*

Some people think they are worth a lot of money just because they have it.
—**Fannie Hurst** *Author*

Stock market research was invented to give credit to astrology.
—***Unknown***

Some people talk a lot before they think of something to say.
—**Blake McBurney** *The McBurney Companies*

Some folks wear their halos much too tight.
—***Unknown***

Progress might have been all right once, but it has gone on too long.
—**Ogden Nash** *Humorist*

Profits like sausages...are esteemed most by those who know least what goes into them.
—**Alvin Toffler** *Futurist*

Prediction is very difficult, especially about the future.
—**Niels Bohr** *Physicist*

Politicians and diapers have one thing in common: they should be changed regularly and for the same reason.
—**Unknown**

The minute you get there, you're still here.
—**Paul Childs** *Vistage Speaker*

People often tell me that motivation doesn't last, and I tell them that bathing doesn't either. That's why I recommend it daily.
—**Zig Ziglar** *Trainer*

It's just amazing how long this country has been going to hell without ever having got there.
—**Andy Rooney** *Commentator*

People never lie so much as after fishing, during a war, or before an election.
—**Unknown**

People are living longer than ever before, a phenomenon undoubtedly made necessary by the 30 year mortgage.
—**Doug Larson** *Humorist*

Out of sight is out of mind and out of mind is out of money, honey.
—**Mae West** *Entertainer*

Orville Wright didn't have a pilot's license.
—**Richard Tait** *Cranium*

Only three percent of adults have written goals, and everyone else works for them.
—**Brian Tracy** *Author*

One dog will work; two dogs will play.
—**Rufus Johnson** *Georgia Farmer*

Once you step in elephant manure, you're in the circus forever.
—**Joe Herman Fincher** *Mill Worker*

Nothing in life is so exhilarating as to be shot at without result.
—**Winston Churchill** *Government Leader*

Nobody has to be perfect until you fall in love with them.
—**Donald Phinn** *Vistage Speaker*

I have no regard for money. Aside from its purchasing power, it's completely useless as far as I'm concerned.
—**Alfred Hitchcock** *Film maker*

No one has ever listened themselves out of a job.
—**Lou Holtz** *Football Coach*

No matter how many times you've given birth, it still hurts to be told you have an ugly baby.
—**Jack Kaine** *Vistage Speaker*

Ninety-nine percent of the people in the world are fools and the rest of us are in great danger of contagion.
—**Thornton Wilder** *Author*

Ninety percent of the politicians give the other 10% a bad reputation.
—**Henry Kissinger** *Secretary of State*

Most people don't know what they're doing, and a lot of them are really good at it.
—**George Carlin** *Entertainer*

Ninety-five percent of people make up their own statistics.
—**Unknown**

Never squat with your spurs on.
  —**Texas Proverb**

Neckties strangle clear thinking.
  —**Lin Yutang** *Author*

My opinions may have changed, but not the fact that I am right.
  —**Ashleigh Brilliant** *Humorist*

Most people would rather be in the casket than delivering the eulogy.
  —**Steven Snyder** *Vistage Speaker*

Most people work just hard enough not to get fired and get paid just enough money not to quit.
  —**George Carlin** *Entertainer*

Most people die at the age of 30; they just don't do us the courtesy of laying down.
  —**J. Howard Shelov** *Vistage Speaker*

Money is better than poverty, if only for financial reasons.
  —**Woody Allen** *Entertainer*

Men who wear earrings make great husbands; they've experienced pain and have bought jewelry.
  —**Mikki Williams** *Vistage Speaker*

Money may not buy happiness, but I'd rather cry in a jaguar that on a bus,
  —**Francoise Sagan** *Author*

Many a man owes his success to his first wife and his second wife to his success.
  —**Jim Backus** *Actor*

No more mistakes and you're through.
  —**John Cleese** *Entertainer*

Life is tough, but it's tougher when you're stupid.
—**John Wayne**   *Actor*

Life begins when the kids leave home and the dog dies.
—**Bud Mingledorff**   *Mingledorff's*

Lead me not into temptation. I can find it myself.
—**John Bernal**   *Physicist*

Lazy people have no spare time.
—**Japanese Proverb**

Laziness travels so slowly that Poverty soon overtakes him.
—**Benjamin Franklin**   *Inventor*

Lawsuit n. A machine which you go into as a pig and come out as a sausage.
—**Ambros Bierce**   *Poet*

I've been promoted to middle management. I never thought I'd sink so low.
—**Tim Gould**   *Author*

It's hard for me to get used to these changing times. I can remember when the air was clean and sex was dirty.
—**George Burns**   *Entertainer*

It's easier to throw hand grenades than it is to catch them.
—**Lyndon B. Johnson**   *President*

It is clear that the future holds great opportunities. It also holds pitfalls. The trick will be to avoid the pitfalls, seize the opportunities and be home by 6 o'clock.
—**Woody Allen**   *Entertainer*

Invest in inflation. It's the only thing that will go up.
—**Will Rogers**   *Humorist*

Let's Get Serious About Humor...

Income tax returns are the most imaginative fiction being written today.
—***Herman Woulk*** *Author*

If I had any humility, I would be perfect.
—***Ted Turner*** *Industrialist*

In this business, you either sink or swim, or you don't.
—***David Smith*** *Sculptor*

If all economists were laid end to end they would not reach a conclusion.
—***George Bernard Shaw*** *Author*

In America, anyone can grow up to be President...it's just one of the risks one takes.
—***Adlai Stevenson*** *Governor*

I'm not young enough to know everything.
—***Oscar Wilde*** *Author*

I'm not okay, you're not okay, but that's okay.
—***Elizabeth Kubler-Ross*** *Author*

If you're going to have a breakfast meeting, it should be in bed with a beautiful woman.
—***Gordon White*** *English Tycoon*

If you obey all the rules, you miss all the fun.
—***Katherine Hepburn*** *Actress*

If you drink, don't drive. Don't even putt.
—***Dean Martin*** *Entertainer*

If you don't set goals, you can't regret not reaching them.
—***Yogi Berra*** *Baseball Player*

If you can't measure it, you can't manage it.
—***Robert Kaplan*** *BSC*

If you can't beat them, arrange to have them beaten.
—**George Carlin** *Entertainer*

If the world were a logical place men would ride side-saddle.
—**Rita Mae Brown** *Author*

If life were fair, Elvis would be alive and all the impersonators would be dead.
—**Johnny Carson** *Entertainer*

If I had my life to live again I'd make the same mistakes - only sooner.
—**Tallulah Bankhead** *Entertainer*

If God wanted us to vote he would have given us candidates.
—**Jim Hightower** *Populist*

If Columbus had an advisory board, he would probably still be on the dock.
—**Arthur J. Goldberg** *Secretary of Labor*

Misers are no fun to live with, but they make great ancestors.
—**Tom Snyder** *Broadcaster*

If a woman has to choose between catching a fly ball and saving an infant's life she will choose to save the infant's life without even considering if there is a man on base.
—**Dave Barry** *Humorist*

I'm more concerned about the return of my money than a return on my money.
—**Will Rogers** *Humorist*

I want to live my life so that when I die they don't have to call a temp agency for pallbearers.
—**Gregory Edwards**

Let's Get Serious About Humor...

I think we consider too much the good luck of the early bird and not enough the bad luck of the early worm.
—**Franklin D. Roosevelt** *President*

I really don't know what I want from life but I'm pretty sure it ain't what I've got.
—**Alfred E. Newman** *Cartoon Character*

Giving money and power to government is like giving whiskey and car keys to teenage boys.
—**P.J. O'Rourke** *Civil Libertarian*

I love mankind, it's people I can't stand.
—**Charles Schulz** *Cartoonist*

I love deadlines. I like the swooshing sound they make as they fly by.
—**Douglas Adams** *Author*

I know that there are people in this world who do not love their fellow man and I hate people like that.
—**Tom Lehrer** *Satirist*

I knew this time would come, but yesterday I didn't know it would be today.
—**Unknown**

I have noticed that people who are late are so often much jollier than the people who have to wait for them.
—**E.V. Lucas** *Essayist*

I have never killed a man, but I have read many obituaries with a lot of pleasure.
—**Clarence Darrow** *Attorney*

I figure if my kids are alive at the end of the day, I've done my job.
—**Roseanne Barr** *Entertainer*

Confidence is like going after Moby Dick with a rowboat, a harpoon and a jar of tartar sauce.
—**Bob Orben**   *Humorist*

I don't want to play golf. When I hit a ball I want somebody else to go chase it.
—**Rogers Hornsby**   *Baseball Player*

I don't want to achieve mortality through my work. I want to achieve it through not dying.
—**Woody Allen**   *Entertainer*

I don't know who first discovered water but I'm pretty sure it wasn't a fish.
—**Marshall McLuhan**   *Author*

I do not object to people looking at their watches while I am talking but I strongly object when they start shaking them to make certain they are still going.
—**Lord Birkett**   *Jurist*

I believe in looking reality straight in the eye and denying it.
—**Garrison Keillor**   *Humorist*

A committee is a group that keeps minutes and loses hours.
—**Milton Berle**   *Comedian*

Hard work never killed anybody, but why take a chance?
—**Charlie McCarthy**   *Entertainer*

Good judgment comes from experience and a lot of that comes from bad judgment.
—**Will Rogers**   *Humorist*

Good bankers, like good tea, can only be appreciated when they are in hot water.
—**Jaffar Hussein**   *Malaysian Central Bank*

Football is a mistake. It combines the two worst elements of American life: violence and committee meetings.
　　—George Will　*Journalist*

Ignorance is not an opinion.
　　—Dilbert　*Cartoon Character*

Expecting the world to treat you fairly because you're a good person is like expecting a bull not to attack because you are a vegetarian.
　　—Dennis Wholey　*Author*

Exhilaration is that feeling you get just after a great idea hits you and just before you realize what's wrong with it.
　　—Unknown

Everyone is entitled to their own opinions. But they are not entitled to their own facts.
　　—Daniel Patrick Moynihan　*Senator*

Everyone here brings happiness: some when they come and some when they leave.
　　—Huldah Mingledorff　*Millhaven Plantation*

Even if you're on track you'll get run over if you just sit there.
　　—Will Rogers　*Humorist*

Even Betty Crocker burns a cake now and then.
　　—Bill Claudill　*Baseball Player*

Even a pancake has two sides.
　　—Griff Griffies　*Vistage Chairman*

Don't trust nobody but your mama, and even then look at her real good.
　　—Bo Diddley　*Musician*

In times like these, it helps to recall that there have always been times like these.
—*Paul Harvey* *Commentator*

Don't say 'yes' until I finish talking.
—*Darryl Zanuck* *Film Executive*

Don't confuse fame with success. Madonna is one; Helen Keller is the other.
—*Erma Bombeck* *Columnist*

Anyone could lead perfect people if there were any.
—*Robert K. Grenleaf* *Philosopher*

Don't vote. You'll only encourage them.
—*Unknown*

Deep down, we're all shallow.
—*Charles Lipman* *DiversiTech*

Criminal: a person with predatory instincts who has not sufficient capital to form a corporation.
—*Howard Scott*

Borrow money from pessimists - they don't expect it back.
—*Steven Wright* *Humorist*

Checking up on a person after delegating authority to them is like pulling a plant out of the ground to see how the roots are doing.
—*Unknown*

Capitalism does not raise all boats; it raises all yachts.
—*Jeffrey Gates* *Shared Capitalism Institute*

Bankruptcy is a legal proceeding in which you put your money in your pants pocket and give your coat to your creditors.
Samuel Goldwyn *Businessman*

Let's Get Serious About Humor…

Business isn't like a box of chocolates. It's more like a jar of jalapenos. What you do today, might burn your butt tomorrow.
—**Larry the Cable Guy**   *Entertainer*

Baseball players are a lot smarter than football players. How often do you see a baseball team penalized for too many men on the field?
—**Jim Bouton**   *Baseball Player*

Bankers are the largest class of unpunished criminals in the country.
—**J. Howard Shelov**   *Vistage Speaker*

As a nation we are dedicated to keeping physically fit - and parking as close to the stadium as possible.
—**Bill Vaughn**   *Columnist*

Always do right. It will please some people and astonish the rest.
—**Mark Twain**   *Humorist*

All I ask is a chance to prove that money can't make me happy.
—**Spike Milligan**   *Entertainer*

A word to the wise ain't necessary; it's the stupid ones who need the advice.
— **Bill Cosby**   *Entertainer*

A rising tide is wonderful if you have a boat.
—**Barney Frank**   *Congressman*

The trouble with quotes on the internet is that it's difficult to determine whether or not they are genuine.
—**Abraham Lincoln**   *President*

Chairman Carter's Volume X

A positive attitude may not solve all your problems but it will annoy enough people to make it worth the effort.
—**Herm Albright** *Artist*

A person who is nice to you but rude to the waiter is not a nice person.
—**Dave Barry** *Humorist*

A mission statement is defined as "a long, awkward sentence that demonstrates management's inability to think clearly." All good companies have one.
—**Dilbert** *Cartoon Character*

A bachelor is a selfish, undeserving guy who has cheated some woman out of a divorce.
—**Don Quinn** *Author*

A lot of fellows nowadays have a B.A., M.D., or Ph.D. Unfortunately, they don't have a J.O.B.
—**Fats Domino** *Entertainer*

A government which robs Peter to pay Paul can always depend on the support of Paul.
—**George Bernard Shaw** *Author*

A cynic is a man who, when he smells flowers, looks around for a coffin.
—**Henry Louis Mencken** *Humorist*

A real executive goes around with a worried look on his direct reports.
—**Unknown**

That's all folks!
—**Porky Pig** *Cartoon Character*

Index

Abbey, Edward 153
Abeel, Bill 167
Ackerman, Charles 66
Adams, Douglas 163, 175
Adams, Scott 166
Adizes, Ichak 4
Adler, Alfred 83
Adler, Fred 5
Aesop 29
Affleck, Mark 118
Aiken, Howard 117
Albrecht, Karl 156
Albright, Herm 180
Aleichem, Sholem 113
Ali, Mohammad 128
Allen, Woody 51, 163, 171, 172, 176
Allison, Malcolm 10
Amos, Daniel 96
Anderson, Chris 52
Anderson, Joe 151
Andretti, Mario 137
Anthony, Robert 32
Arden, Ron 72
Armstrong, Louis 93
Arvin, David 127
Ash, Mary Kay 116
Ashe, Arthur 114
Astor, Brooke 154
Atlee, Clement 34
Austin, Dean 11
Back, Richard 118
Backus, Jim 171
Baldwin, James 139
Balentine, Robert 30, 94

Bankhead, Tallulah 174
Banks, Dr. Murray 164
Banks, Harry F. 48
Bardwick, Judith 39
Barker, Joel A. 9, 138
Barnes, Tony 88
Barnett, Dan 4, 31, 108
Barr, Roseanne 51, 175
Barrie, James, M. 64
Barry, Dave 174, 180
Basch, Michael 14, 72, 108, 140
Beans, Jason 76
Beaulieu, Brian 46, 85, 93, 154
Bench, Johnny 152
Benfield, John 29
Bennis, Warren 3, 6, 43, 103, 147
Berenson, Bernard 31
Berg, Deanna 11, 33, 65, 70
Berger, Thomas 67
Berle, Milton 176
Bermard, Charles 65
Bernal, John 172
Bernstein, Al 107
Berra, Yogi 44, 113, 173
Berry, Leonard 86
Bethune, Gordon 28
Bezos, Jeff 106, 114
Bierce, Ambros 172
Bilbey, Walter 129
Billings, Josh 58
Birkett, Lord 176
Blackman, Jeff 75, 87, 103
Blackwell, Roger 6, 82, 85
Blanchard, Ken 42, 65, 109
Blank, Arthur 96
Blanton, Bill 34

Index

Blau, Emile 151
Bleech, Jim 8, 88
Blessington, Lady Maguerite 52
Bloody Mary 113
Blumenthal, Ira 10
Bohm, David 92
Bohr, Niels 169
Bok, Derek 61
Bombeck, Erma 178
Bonaparte, Napoleon 15, 133
Borden, William 125
Borreson, David 83, 109
Bortree, Paul 84
Bossidy, Lawrence 11
Bouton, Jim 179
Bowden, Bobby 126
Bowers, Sam 3, 8, 14, 15, 71, 88, 94
Bradbury, Ray 88, 96
Bradford, Arthur William 75
Brandeis, Louis 87
Brandon, Dick 142
Braude, Jacob M. 40
Breier, Bruce 14, 106
Brien, Richard H. 143
Brilliant, Ashleigh 171
Brinkley, David 46
British Military Commander 42
Brokaw, Tom 42, 139
Brooks, Bill 124, 126
Broun, Heywood 43
Brown, Charlie 83, 156
Brown, Edmund G. 150
Brown, Prof. Ray E. 64, 104
Brown, Rita Mae 91, 174
Buffet, Warren 3, 11, 58, 61, 82, 156
Bumper Sticker 124

Burback, Larry 96
Burns, George 123, 172
Bushnell, Nolan 59
Bustin, Greg 21, 77
Butler, Samuel 36
Byrnes, James F. 50
Cabell, James Branch 127
Calhoun, David 16, 29
Calloway, D. Wayne 3
Campbell, Joseph 157
Canic, Michael 3, 7, 15, 61, 130, 131
Capone, Al 163
Carey, Max 49, 64, 103
Cargill, Gil 3, 47, 66, 81, 108
Carlin, George 170, 171, 174
Carlzon, Jan 11, 57
Carson, Johnny 174
Carter, Bud 15, 44, 94
Carter, Hodding 104
Carter, Rosalynn 75
Cash, Johnny 119
Cass, Lewis 108
Casten, Sean 14
Cathy, Truett 15, 83
Cecil, Jim 9, 15, 19, 36, 39, 68, 69, 138
Chamberlain, Wilt 153
Chanel, Coco 88, 117
Chaney, Fred 66
Charell, Ralph 132
Charles, C. Leslie 28
Chartier, Emile 86
Chase, Ilka 163
Chekhov, Anton 37
Childs, Paul 111, 169
Chinese Fortune Cookie 95
Churchill, Winston 15, 34, 49, 67, 105, 114, 124, 143, 155, 170

Cischke, Susan 124
Clafford, Patricia 126
Clarke, Arthur C. 154
Claudill, Bill 177
Cleese, John 171
Cleveland, Bob 59
Cobb, Bill 20
Cobb, Irving S. 69
Coggins, Bud 89
Cole, David 133
Cole, Ken 110
Colins, Dr. Joseph 76
Collins, Jim 90, 92, 129, 151
Collins, John Churton 38
Collins, Peter 46, 155
Comcast advertising slogan, ... 136
Connellan, Thomas K. 49
Cook, Dick 35
Cooke, Alistair 76
Cookerly, Carol 101
Coolidge, Calvin 59, 64
Coriell, Pete 137
Cosby, Bill 179
Cotrozolla, Joe 28
Courteline, Georges 114
Courtney, Henry 152
Covey, Stephen R. 86, 95, 127
Coward, Noel 52
Crook, James 105
Crow, Trammel 48
Crubman, Dr. James 138
Crupi, James 19
Cutler, Laurel 15
Da Vinci, Leonardo 31
Dabic, Bob 64
Daly, Jack 5, 19

D'Amato, Cus 47
Darrow, Clarence 128, 175
Darwin, Charles 83
Davis, J.E. 20
Davis, Stan 44, 147
Davis, Stanley 138
De Gaulle, Charles 45, 144
De Labruyere, Jean 70
DeBoer, Jack 10
Dell, Bruce 80
Dell, Michael 80, 126
Deming, W. Edwards 20, 89, 133
Dempsey, Val 22, 114, 123
Dent, Harry 66
Depew, Chauncey 114
DePree, D.J. 136
DePree, Herman 76
Desatnick, Bob 58
Detienne, Rick 116
Deutsch, Barry 111
Dickerson, Richard 46
Diddley, Bo 177
Dilbert 51, 78, 180
Dillon, Joe 143
Dirksen, Everett 79
Disney, Walt 35, 163
Ditka, Mike 88
Dole, Robert 11
Domino, Fats 180
Dos Passos, John 87
Dr. Suess 159
Drucker, Peter .. 4, 9, 10, 13, 18, 19, 20, 23, 36, 40, 51, 66, 68, 97, 101, 106, 130, 144, 154, 156
Dulles, John Foster 48, 128
Dumas, Alexander 60
Duncan, Al 78

Index

Durant, William 79
Duryee, Dave 22
Dushoff, Lee 159
Earp, Wyatt 23
Easterling, Barry 125
Eban, Abba 72
Edison, Thomas 41, 107, 157
Edwards, Gregory 135, 174
Einstein, Albert 9, 40, 61, 79, 80, 81, 90, 92
Eisenhower Gen. Dwight D. 6, 14, 82, 124
Eisner, Michael 14
Eliot, George 111
Ellery, Bob 7
Ellison, Larry 114
Emerson, Ralph Waldo 37, 104
Emmerich, Roxanne 115
England, Terry 136
Erben, James 7
Exupery, Antoine St. 112
Fallon, Brad 79, 112
Faust, Gerry 14, 90, 91, 106, 107, 108, 123, 138, 144, 158
Favitch, Diane 101
Favizza, Ken 134
Feather, Leonard 9
Federighi, Craig 78
Fehrman, Garry 77
Feltenstein, Tom 18, 34, 111, 112, 132, 133, 136, 137
Fey, Tina 82
Fields, Mark 10
Fields, Marshall 58, 65
Fields, W.C. 168
Fincher, Joe Herman 170
Fincher, Lois 137
Firestone, Harvey 20
Fisher, Carrie 93
Fisher, George M.C. 84

Fisher, Jeff 10
Flamholtz, Eric 29
Flanders, Scott 7
Fleisher, Ron 67
Fleming, Andy 30, 57, 155
Flinn, Pat 20
Flom, Edward L 44
Floyd, Bert 111
Forbes Magazine 52
Forbes, B.C. 159
Forbes, Malcolm 40, 113, 137, 141, 143
Ford, Gerald 144, 165
Ford, Henry 7, 11, 29, 52, 57, 59, 87, 108, 118
Forencich, Frank 167
Forsee, Vincent 14
Foster, E.M. 87, 88
Foster, Mike 39
Francis, Clarence 71, 152
Franck, James 128
Frank, Barney 179
Franklin, Benjamin 57, 75, 172
Fraser, Don 89
Freidman, Thomas 141
Fretz, Randy 7, 31
Friedman, Bob 137
Frost, Robert 28, 30, 141, 168
Fuller, Buckminster 51
Fuller, Thomas 11, 34
Galbraith, John Kenneth 85, 116
Gandhi, Mahatma 78, 127
Garcia, Jerry 107
Gates, Bill 34, 53, 129, 131
Gates, Jeffrey 178
Geary, Joe 30
Gerber, Michael 13, 50, 134
Getty, J. Paul 63, 81, 83, 93, 115, 167

Index

Gibbs, Joe ... 86
Gibers, Dr. Lydia ... 128
Gibson, Bob ... 135
Gibson, William ... 126
Gill, , Vince ... 47
Gilmer, Henry ... 110
Glasgow, Ellen ... 123
Glasow, Arnold ... 41
Glassman, James K. ... 116
Godin, Seth ... 142
Goizueta, Robert ... 13
Goldberg, Arthur J. ... 174
Goldberg, Barney ... 19
Goldberg, Harvey ... 48
Goldratt, Eli ... 52
Goldress, Jerry ... 7, 11, 14, 22, 67, 79, 86, 94, 107
Goldwyn, Samuel ... 13, 139, 178
Goodhue, Alan ... 155
Gooze, Mitch ... 39, 78, 84, 101
Gould, Tim ... 172
Gracian, Baltasar ... 148
Graffito ... 167
Graham, Bill ... 101
Graham, John R. ... 70
Graham, Katherine ... 154
Gray, Albert E.N. ... 52
Green, Harold ... 82
Greenbank, Anthony ... 11
Greenspan, Allan ... 33
Grenleaf, Robert K. ... 178
Gretzky, Wayne ... 101, 159
Griffies, Griff ... 177
Grimes, Richard ... 165
Grizzard, Lewis ... 35
Grothe, Dr. Mardy ... 62, 95, 110, 131
Grove, Andy ... 9

Gwynn, Tony 45
Haab, Richard 45
Hadden, Richard 10
Half, Robert 59, 114
Hamel, Gary 103
Hammarskjold, Dag 22
Hamson, Ned 53
Hankey, Don 9
Hanks, Chris 46
Hanson, David 4, 84, 115
Hanson, Richard 92
Hardin, Jack 12
Harnishe, Verne 37
Harriman, Edward H. 85
Harris, Sidney J. 109
Harty, Steve 113
Harvey, Dr. Jerry 4, 33, 140
Harvey, Paul 33, 139, 178
Haskins, Henry S. 36, 95
Hastings, Reed 13, 69
Hastings, Robert J. 153
Hauseman, David 20
Hayes, Woody 22
Hayward Daily Review 69, 124, 129
Hazlitt, William 50
Heine, Henrich 12
Heller, Stuart 104
Hellman, Karl 63
Hellman, Lillian 152
Helms, Dr. Wayne 112
Hemingway, Ernest 88
Hendricks, Timothy 41
Hennessy, Edward 59
Henrichs, Garth 91
Hepburn, Katherine 173
Herman, Fred 19

Hesburgh, Father Theodore 93
Hightower, Cullen 141
Hightower, Jim 174
Hill, George 42
Hill, Napoleon 47, 156
Hill, Vernon 60
Hilton, Conrad 67
Hitchcock, Alfred 93, 170
Hoc D. 93
Hodgson, Ralph 167
Hoffer, Eric 61, 94
Holmes, John Andrew 130
Holmes, Oliver Wendell 41, 68
Holtz, Lou 128, 130, 141, 170
Honold, Linda 37, 41, 96
Hoover, Herbert 119
Hopper, Grace 160
Horn, Skip 87
Hornsby, Rogers 176
Houle, David 22, 76
Hseih, Tony 80
Hubbard, Elbert 70, 90
Hubbard, Kin 97
Hurdle, Clint 95
Hurst, Fannie 168
Hussein, Jaffar 176
Hutchens, Amy K. 27, 65, 95, 119
Huxley, Aldous 141
Hwang, Dr Terresa 129
Hyden, Howard 12, 22, 39, 76, 94, 117
Hynes, Stanley 68
Iacocca, Lee 150, 153
Irish Blessing 57
Irving, Washington 124
Jacknis, Marty 107, 149
Jackson, Austen 3

191

James, William 152
Jaquith, Andrew 35
Jay, Anthony 104
Jefferson, Thomas 63
Jeremiah, Simon 103
Jerrold, Douglas 110
Jetha, Akbarali 88
Jobs, Steve 21
John XXIII, Pope 108
Johnson, Clark 29, 51, 90, 110, 114
Johnson, Dr. Michael 81
Johnson, Kimberly 109
Johnson, Lyndon B. 22, 172
Johnson, Rufus 169
Joplin, Janis 34
Joubert, Joseph 76
Kafka, Franz 32
Kaine, Jack 4, 58, 61, 62, 65, 66, 91, 170
Kaiser, Harry 147
Kaplan, Robert 173
Karr, Alphonse 42
Katz, Lee 13
Kay, John 13
Kaye, Danny 134
Keats, John 151
Keillor, Garrison 176
Kelleher, Herb 27, 62
Kelly, Ken 40
Kemp, Jan 14
Kennedy, John F. 29, 63, 125
Kennedy, Robert F. 14, 123, 132
Kerkorian, Kirk 80
Kettering, Charles F. 117, 133
Keynes, John Maynard 90
Kiam, Victor 42
Kierkegaard, Soren 134

Index

King, Charlie 6, 32, 138, 158
King, Larry 19, 68
Kiser, Walt 32
Kissinger, Henry 104, 170
Knecht, Larry 142
Knight, Bobby 70
Knox, Chuck 153
Knudsen, William S. 61
Kopelman, Richard 48
Koppel, Ted 108
Korda, Michael 53
Kornfield, Dr. Jerry 71, 137, 141
Korzybski, Alfred 51
Kotter, Prof. John 110
Koufax, Sandy 165
Kramers, Kraig 3, 54, 77, 85, 92, 117
Kravitz, Steve 140
Krida, Jeffrey 128
Kritzer, David 106
Kroc, Ray 36, 60, 150
Kubler-Ross, Elizabeth 173
Lakin, Duane 27
Langley, Vince 7, 119
Laoruangroch. Brian 59
Larry the Cable Guy 179
Larson, Doug 95, 166, 169
Lasorda, Tommy 20, 39
Law, Vernon 141
Lawless, Alessandra 107
Lawrence, D.H. 53
Laws, Arthur P. 163
Layo, Gerry 23, 33, 61, 115
LeBoeuf, Michael 41, 63, 130
Lee, Harper 46
Lee, John 28, 123
Lee, Robert E 58

Lehrer, Tom 36, 175
Leider, Richard 47
Lencioni, Patrick 48
Levenson, Sam 50
Levinson, Jay 22
Levitt, Ted 20
Lewis, C.S. 85
Lientz, Jim 81
Lincoln, Abraham 35, 158, 179
Lindsay, John V. 49
Link, Henry G. 112
Lipman, Charles 22, 27, 96, 104, 135, 178
Lippmann, Walter 124
Logan, David 102
Lombardi, Vince 30, 35, 91
London, Jack 157
Loomis, Bernard 92
Lore, Mary 94
Lotito, Michael 61, 143, 148
Lott, Hunter 6, 9, 113
Lucas, E.V. 175
Luger, Donald 64, 135
Luther, Martin 41, 141
MacDougall, Ian 132
Machiavelli 16
Mackay, Harvey 21, 150
Madrid, Jim 155
Maguire, Frank 23, 40, 49, 60, 70, 83, 89, 102, 118
Maister, David 103
Malherbe, Gideon 23, 36, 86, 157
Malik, Om 8
Manfouz, Naguib 118
Manuel, Jerry 23
Marbury, Elisabeth 91
Marcus, Bernard 8
Marcus, John 67

Marcus, Stanley *23*
Marden, Luis *132*
Markle, Gary *62, 103, 156*
Marquis, Don *66*
Marriott, J.W. *6, 62*
Martin, Dean *173*
Martin, Steve *50*
Martzall, Kirby *18, 133*
Marx, Chico *164*
Marx, Karl *130*
Mascarenhas, Maurice *31, 33, 37, 45, 81, 116, 142, 143*
Masterson, Bat *49*
Maugham W. Somerset *155*
Maxwell, John *23, 160*
McAloon, T.A. *33*
McArthur, Peter *116*
McBurney, Blake *168*
McBurney, William *150*
McCart, Jeff *23*
McCarthy, Charlie *176*
McCartney, Paul *49*
McCourt, Malachy *130*
McGeady, Sister Mary Rose *54*
McGovern, George *45*
McGriff, Michael *58*
McKinnon, Lauch *21, 75*
McLuhan, Marshall *133, 176*
McMurtry, Larry *92*
McNeil, John *4*
McNemey, Jim *31*
McWhirter, Bob *65*
Meek, Catherine *10, 50, 77*
Meenan, Karen *49*
Meli, Vynnie *96*
Mellor, David *95*
Mencken, Henry Louis *20, 48, 180*

Meredith, Don 167
Meyer, Herb 22, 40, 57, 140
Midas, Mike 102
Mikkelson, Barbara 71
Milken, Michael 71
Miller, Irwin 6
Miller, Wiley 129
Milligan, Spike 179
Milteer, Lee 89
Mingledorff, Bud 8, 9, 16, 28, 69, 108, 131, 172
Mingledorff, Huldah 177
Mingledorff, Lee 43
Mingus, Charles 118
Minuto, Dean 61, 101, 129
Monaghan, Tom 39
Monroe, Marilyn 27
Moore, Hannah 132
Moore, Malcolm 65, 79
Morgan, Randy 18
Morita, Akio 50
Morley, Christopher 93
Morris, Tom 159
Mosley, Eric 78
Mother Teresa 132, 158
Moynihan, Daniel Patrick 177
Muchnick, Marc 53
Muggeridge, Malcom 85
Mulling, Emory 18
Mulvaney, Maureen 160
Murchison, Clint 48
Murdoch, Rupert 18, 143
Murray, Donald 104
Murray, J.P. 87
Murray, Jim 44
Murray, Mike 109
Murray, Pat 10, 18, 36, 47, 68, 124

Index

Murrow, Edward R. 19, 90
Myers, Kevin 105
Naddaff, George 29
Nader, Ralph 32
Namath, Joe 147
Nanus, Burt 147, 156
Narasin, Ben 18
Nash, Ogden 168
Nashville Vistage Member 37
Neal, John 75
Nehru 6
Nerenberg, Lowell 135
Nesbit, John 75
Neuharth, Al 142
Newman, Alfred E. 175
Newmark, Craig 155
Newton, James 19, 69, 71, 151
Nicholson, Jack 163
Nicklaus, Jack 60
Niella, Reinaldo 43
Nightingale, Earl 154
Nixon, Richard 138
Noble, Charles C. 123
Noonan, Peggy 165
O'Neill, Eugene 126
Ogilvie, David 76, 157
Ohmae, Konichi 150
O'Neill, Jessie 102
Orben, Bob 168
O'Rourke, P.J. 47, 175
Osgood, Charles 93
Ozley, Lee 8
Pagano, Barbara 84
Page, Arthur W. 160
Paige, Satchel 60
Palmer, Richard 16, 19, 79, 91, 115, 151

Panos, Pierre *39*
Parasuraman, A. *86*
Parcels, Bill *112*
Parilla, Ralph *18*
Parker, Col. Tom *78, 163*
Parker, Dorothy *164*
Parker, Mike *78*
Parker, Sam *104*
Parker, Tom *128*
Parsons, Richard *115*
Parton, Dolly *166*
Paterno, Joe *131*
Patrick, Danica *18*
Patterson, Bob *8*
Patton, Gen. George *54*
Paulson, Dr. Terry *112, 136*
Penney, J.C. *126*
Pensa, Marisa *128, 156*
Perdue, Frank *57*
Perkins, John *92*
Perot, H. Ross *63, 78, 112*
Peter, Laurence J. *28, 34, 37, 52, 109, 160, 167*
Peters, Tom *30, 46, 47, 66, 70, 81, 84, 85, 108, 127, 148*
Peterson, Donald *80*
Peterson, Jeff *68*
Pew, Bob *126*
Phillips, Wesley *119*
Phillips, Will *8, 21*
Phinn, Donald *12, 66, 101, 138, 170*
Picasso *147*
Pickens, T. Boone *163*
Pine, Joe *153*
Pine, Joseph *29*
Plato *30, 103, 124*
Pogo *94*
Poling, Del *21, 134*

Porky Pig *180*
Posada, Jorge *21*
Postman, Neil *79*
Powell, Gen. Colin *65, 96*
Pravda, Susan *125*
Presley, Elvis *148*
Price, Michael *53*
Price, Pat *152*
Pritchett, Price *130*
Prosen, Bob *12, 38, 127*
Proverb, African *87*
Proverb, Arabian *59, 75*
Proverb, Chinese *138*
Proverb, Eskimo *53*
Proverb, Irish *53*
Proverb, Japanese *172*
Proverb, Texas *171*
Proverb, Yiddish *71*
Quinn, Don *180*
Ramsey, Dave *12*
Rand, Ayn *45*
Randall, Clarence B. *8*
Randall, Stanley J. *106*
Rankin, Jeanette *101*
Ravitch, Diane *91*
Reagan, Ronald *42, 45, 166, 167*
Reaves, Chuck *37, 40, 45, 54, 65, 77, 95, 105, 149*
Refinbary, Jay *17, 18, 40*
Remillard, Brad *12, 101, 133*
Restaurant chain slogan *147*
Retiring GM worker *59*
Rheem, Don *58*
Rhoades, Ann *69*
Rice, John *21*
Richard, Rick *153*
Richards, Paul *17*

Richardson, Curt 44
Richardson, Mike 78, 104
Rickey, Branch 110
Rickover, Adm. Hyman 115, 142, 160
Riis, Jacob 38
Rizowy, Carlos 125, 128, 147
Rockefeller, John D. 8, 10, 80
Roddick, Anita 64
Rodman, Frances 135
Rodnick, Richard 4
Rodriquez, Robert 4, 136
Rogers, Morgan 147
Rogers, Will 33, 148, 150, 164, 165, 166, 172, 174, 176, 177
Rohn, Jim 50, 131, 149
Rommel, Erwin 17
Romney, George 148
Rooney, Andy 134, 169
Roosevelt, Eleanor 30, 133
Roosevelt, Franklin D. 130, 175
Rose, Lynn 27
Rosen, Leonard 133
Ross, Eliza Patton 30
Roth, John 165
Rousseau 151
Roux, Joseph 57
Rowe, Ron 57, 60
Ruff, Howard 111
Rukeyser, Louis 135
Ruland, Mike 77
Rumans, Dr. Mark 12
Rumsfeld, Donald 9
Ruscio, Ken 35
Ruskin, John 106
Russell, Bertrand 46, 117
Rutherford, Johnny 68
Ryan, Ed 21, 83, 89, 131, 140

Sagan, Francoise	171
Saint Teresa of Avila	131
Sanborn, Mark	59
Sanchez, Abe	21, 77, 91
Sandberg, Sheryl	13
Sanders, Barry	102
Sanders, Don A.	142
Sandstrom, Jim	153
Santayana, George	125, 126
Sarnoff, David	117
Sarnoff, Dorothy	155
Schimel, Barry	144
Schmidt, Eric	68
Schmincke, Don	21, 38, 42, 95, 105, 135, 150, 159
Schneider, Vicki	5
Schuller, Robert H.	125
Schulz, Charles	134, 175
Schulze, Horst	66
Schutz, Peter	22, 23, 57, 60, 75, 81, 82, 83, 130, 148, 149
Schwab, Charles	75
Schwarz, Bill	62, 85, 113, 147
Scott, Howard	178
Scott, Red	28, 32, 44, 62, 101, 137, 158
Scott, Susan	106
Scully, Vin	46
Searcy, Tom	33, 63, 68, 102
Sechrest, Lee	38
Seeger, Pete	117
Sellers, Peter	115
Sertillanges, A.G.	105
Sessoms, Walt	34
Setchell, Nick	52
Seydel, Scott	48
Shamis, Barry	36, 46, 69
Shaw, George Bernard	173, 180

Shechtman, Morrie 29, 48, 61, 63, 87, 97, 102, 113, 119, 144, 150, 154
Sheinberg, Sheila 148
Shelov, J. Howard 54, 89, 171, 179
Shiely, John 17
Shoemaker, Willie 152
Shore, Joe 37
Shorten, Dick 111
Siedlick, Larry 159
Sign in Kentucky field 136
Sign in Nordstrom employee lounge 149
Sign in S.C. Restaurant 127
Sign in Tucson coffee house 142
Sign, US Navy Seals Training Center 90
Silva, Jose 107
Simanek, Donald 153
Simon, Neil 27
Skinner, B.F. 47
Smith, David 173
Smith, Fred 119
Smith, Hiram 77
Smith, Jaynie 3, 38, 42, 89
Smith, Logan Piersall 149
Smith, Martin Cruze 160
Smith, Scott 19
Smith, Stan 158
Smithgall, Charles 82, 139
Snow, Dennis 5
Snyder, Charlie 43
Snyder, Steve 80, 124, 147
Snyder, Steven 29, 91, 93, 105, 113, 140, 142, 171
Snyder, Tom 174
Soden, Allen 50
Sonduck, Michael 71
Sorrell, Scott 30
Spence, Gerry 43

Spoor, William *159*
Spurgeon, Charles Haddon *111*
Stack, Jack *17*
Stadler, Rupert *9*
Stahl, Sheldon *140*
Starr, Judith *39*
Stassen, Harold *139*
Stayer, Ralph *142*
Stein, George *102*
Stein, Gertrude *79, 155*
Stein, Herbert *5*
Steinbrenner, George *53*
Steinem, Gloria *127*
Stengel, Casey *42, 92*
Sterman, John D. *94*
Stevens, Wallace *88*
Stevenson, Adlai *28, 173*
Stevenson, Howard *28*
Stevenson, Robert Louis *158*
Stiritz, William *69*
Stone, W. Clement *107*
Stratman, Scott *105*
Stutman, Robert *126*
Sulkowicz, Kerry *12*
Sullivan, Dan *82*
Sutton, Bob *70*
Sutton, Robert *5*
Sutton, Walt *79, 111*
Suzuki, D.T. *62*
Taggart, Bob *157*
Tait, Richard *64, 169*
Taleb, Nassim *90*
Talmadge, Betty *27*
Talmud, The *70*
Taylor-Klaus, David *17, 86*
Techsonic *150*

Tedlow, Richard 129
Teel, Gordon 112
Teerlink, Richard 10, 64
Thatcher, Margaret 31, 33
Thayer, Lee 87, 153
Thomas, Bob 143
Thomson, Bob 12, 51, 110
Thurber, James 84, 96
Toffler, Alvin 157, 168
Tomlin, Lily 32, 123, 166
Townsend, Robert 155
Toynbee, Arthur 105
Tracy, Brian 42, 156, 169
Truman, Harry 102, 129, 135
Trump, Donald 118
Tse, Lao 164
Tunstall, Gordon 81, 85
Tupper, M.T. 50
Turner, Ted 173
Twain, Mark 110, 115, 134, 164, 165, 179
Tweed, Boss 62
Twiford, Bortie 139
Tyabji, Hatim 45
Tyson, Mike 7
Tzu, Lao 67
Tzu, Sun 17, 67
Ueberroth, Peter 34
Ulrich, Laurel Thatcher 49
Unidentified Stanford Economics Professor 43
Vabulas, Andy 10, 31
Valentine, Bill 40
Van Hooser, Phillip 83, 84
Van Roden, Trip 16
Vance, Donald R. 118
Vanderpoel, Robert P. 51
Varian, Russel 116

Index

Vaughn, Bill 179
Vent, The 32
Vidal, Gore 151
Vitale, Joe 13
Vogelsang, Jeff 5, 136, 139
Voltaire 31, 62
Von Braun, Wernher 27, 165
Vonnegut, Kurt 76
vos Savant, Marilyn 141
Wachner, Linda 127
Wagner, Bill 38
Walden, Russ 8, 17, 35, 38, 43, 80, 114, 123, 131, 152
Waldrip, Mary 111
Walker, James J. 119
Walton, Sam 114
Ward Beecher, Henry 103
Warhol, Andy 118
Warren, Rick 90
Washington, Booker 116
Watson, Thomas 69, 96
Watterson, Bill 62
Wayne, John 12, 168, 172
Weaver, Bob 49, 125, 149
Weber, Bob 159
Weber, Craig 152
Weiler, A.H. 109
Weiss, Alan 82
Welch, Jack 5, 17, 31, 110, 137, 139
Wells, Leo 35, 115, 127, 138, 148
Wertenberg, Dan 60, 118
West, Mae 50, 169
Westcott, Katherine 28
Whisenhunt, Livia 86
White, E.B. 151
White, Gordon 173
White, Leon 157

White, Slappy 166
Wholey, Dennis 177
Wigley, Clark 17, 38
Wilcox, Frederick 108
Wilde, Oscar 39, 125, 127, 173
Wilder, Billy 147
Wilder, Thornton 170
Wiley, Steve 63
Wilkinson, Tim 80
Will, George 16, 41, 129, 135, 177
Williams, Joseph 125
Williams, Mikki 171
Williams, Ted 136
Williams, Tennessee 71
Wilson, Earl 107
Wilson, Flip 41
Wilson, Fred 58
Wilson, Gerald E. 109
Wilson, Kemmons 84
Wilson, Larry 84
Wilson, Woodrow 15
Winchell, Walter 132
Winner, Michael 16
Wise, Dave 80
Wisner, Jim 103
Witte, Dr. Hermann 131
Wolff, Les 110
Wood, Tom 27
Wooden, John 84, 86, 94, 117, 140, 149, 159
Woodruff, Robert 149
Woulk, Herman 173
Wright, John David 142
Wright, Steven 178
Yalom, Irvin 140
Yastrow, Steve 16, 63
Yoho, David 78

Index

Young, Andrew *109*
Yutang, Lin *77, 171*
Zabriskie, Kate *15*
Zakaria, Fareed *15*
Zanuck, Darryl *178*
Zaphiropoulos, Renn *5, 7, 13, 16, 118, 123*
Zen Buddhist maxim *95*
Zen Saying *43*
Ziglar, Zig *6, 71, 156, 169*

We hope you enjoyed

Pithy Quotes

Who do you know who might also enjoy the book?

Pithy Quotes is available for $19.95 (postage included) on Amazon. If you think a compilation of quotes "designed to improve your bottom line" might be a good tool for marketing, customized copies (including your firm's name on the front cover) are available at a significant discount.

For more information, contact:

Bud Carter
budcarter@aol.com